Looking Homeward

Looking Homeward

A Thomas Wolfe Photo Album

Morton I. Teicher

UNIVERSITY OF MISSOURI PRESS   COLUMBIA AND LONDON

Copyright © 1993 by
The Curators of the University of Missouri
University of Missouri Press, Columbia, Missouri 65201
Printed and bound in the United States of America
All rights reserved

5   4   3   2   1   97   96   95   94   93

Library of Congress Cataloging-in-Publication Data

Teicher, Morton I.
    Looking homeward : a Thomas Wolfe photo album / Morton I. Teicher.
      p. cm.
    Includes bibliographical references and index.
    ISBN 0-8262-0893-2 (alk. paper)
    1. Wolfe, Thomas, 1900–1938—Biography—Pictorial works.
  2. Novelists, American—20th century—Biography—Pictorial works.
  I. Title.
  PS3545.0337Z8625   1993
  813'.52—dc20   92-41925
  [B]   CIP

♾™ This paper meets the requirements of the
American National Standard for Permanence of Paper
for Printed Library Materials, Z39.48, 1984.

Designer: Kristie Lee
Typesetter: Connell-Zeko Type & Graphics
Printer and binder: Thomson-Shore, Inc.
Typefaces: Palatino and Tropez Light

To my wife, Mickey, with love

Contents

Acknowledgments

The publication of this book coincides with the golden anniversary of my having "discovered" Thomas Wolfe. In 1943, I was a soldier in the American army beginning what became almost three years of service in the China-Burma-India theater. I happened to come across the armed forces editions of *Look Homeward, Angel* and *Of Time and the River,* and I was profoundly impressed by how Wolfe's eloquent descriptions of loneliness precisely and accurately echoed my innermost feelings at the time. Ever since then, I have been a student and admirer of his work, an author of articles about him, a participant in organizing and maintaining a society devoted to keeping his memory green, and an avid collector of Wolfe material, including photographs. In effect, the preparation of this book has taken a half-century. Throughout these many years, I have received encouragement and support from many wonderful friends to whom I am deeply indebted for having contributed so much to aid me in the preparation of this book.

In 1978, Louis Rubin and I were faculty members at the University of North Carolina at Chapel Hill. He conceived the idea of a pictorial biography of Wolfe and invited my collaboration. When his duties at a new publishing house, Algonquin Press, claimed his time and attention, he generously demonstrated genuine scholarly colleagueship by agreeing that I could proceed independently. I am grateful to this foremost expert on southern literature.

The late Richard Walser of North Carolina State University, an unusual Wolfe scholar, stimulated my interest in

Wolfe generally and my work on this book, in particular. His memory shall always be a blessing to me and to all admirers of Thomas Wolfe's writings.

Since its inception in 1980, the Thomas Wolfe Society has continuously shored up my interest in Wolfe, providing rich opportunities for interaction with like-minded Wolfe fans. I owe thanks to all members of the society, especially to the presidents who preceded and followed me in that office: Duane Schneider, Richard Kennedy, John Idol, Elizabeth Evans, and James Clark. Duane Schneider and James Clark also provided pictures, and John Idol made excellent suggestions for improving the manuscript.

Many people have participated in my endless search for pictures pertaining to Wolfe. Sylvia and Jack Nussbaum and Barbara Mykland sought out sources in the Seattle area. Adele and James Cleary photographed sites of Wolfe interest as they appear today. Marnie and James Haines, Elizabeth Goldman, my granddaughter, and my wife accompanied me on a photo-taking visit to 32 Wellington Square in London, where Wolfe worked on *Look Homeward, Angel* in 1926 and where Patricia Stoughton, owner of the building, welcomed us cordially in 1984.

Paul Gitlin, executor of the Wolfe estate, first granted me access to the Wolfe collections at the University of North Carolina and Harvard University in 1977. Rodney Dennis, Houghton Library, Harvard University, and Alice Cotten and H. G. Jones, University of North Carolina Library, were most cooperative. Jerry Cotten, Photographic Services Division, University of North Carolina Library, was especially helpful.

A major source of my photographs is the Pack Memorial Library, Asheville-Buncombe Library System. Edward Sheary and Philip Blank extended every courtesy to me. AGA Photo Labs meticulously copied the pictures. Also in Asheville, I received assistance from Steve Hill and Ted Mitchell of the Thomas Wolfe Memorial.

Diligent tracking led me to Gwen Ruge Port in Phoenix, Arizona, who kindly provided pictures of her father, Dr. Edward Ruge, and of his sanatorium, Firlawns, near Seattle, where Wolfe was a patient in 1938. A memorable visit to Memphis, Tennessee, in 1988 produced pictures from the extraordinary Braden-Hatchett Thomas Wolfe Collection. The late William Hatchett and his obliging wife, Eva Braden Hatchett, received my wife and me with great kindness and eager collaboration.

Archivists at Johns Hopkins Hospital, Providence Hospital, the University of Washington, and the Mariners' Museum patiently dug into their files to provide pictures.

Aldo Magi is an indefatigable Wolfe collector and scholar.

He is a devoted friend who unstintingly provided me with pictures and identifications from his superb knowledge about Wolfe and from his matchless treasure trove of Wolfeana. His enthusiasm for Wolfe's work is an inspiration to me and to countless others who have been "turned on" to Wolfe by him.

The editors at the University of Missouri Press, Beverly Jarrett and Jane Lago, have been most patient and most constructive in their suggestions.

Pictures, support, and cooperation have come from Clara Stites, daughter of Elizabeth Nowell; Mary Aswell Doll, daughter of Edward Aswell; Paula Maute, Paul Duke, Frank Wilson, Dan Burne Jones, Andrea Brown, and Lou Harshaw.

Finally, I want to express unreserved gratitude to my wife, Mickey Teicher, who has put up with my Wolfe mania during the many years of our long and happy marriage. Most notably, she has persevered through the loneliness of thought, the dreariness of labor, and the ashes of creation that have gone into the making of this book. I lovingly dedicate it to her.

Credits

The following abbreviations are used to indicate the source of each illustration.

Braden-Hatchett	Braden-Hatchett Thomas Wolfe Collection, now at the University of North Carolina Library, Chapel Hill
Brewer	Therese Brewer
Chesney Archives	The Alan Mason Chesney Medical Archives of the Johns Hopkins Medical Institutions, Baltimore, Maryland
Cleary	James C. Cleary
Cultural Resources	North Carolina Department of Cultural Resources, Division of Archives and History, Raleigh
Doll	Mary Aswell Doll
Duke	Collection of Paul M. Duke
Gordon	John Gordon, photographer, Raleigh, North Carolina
Houghton Library	By permission of the Houghton Library, Harvard University, Cambridge, Massachusetts

Magi	Aldo P. Magi Collection of Thomas Wolfe
Mariners' Museum	The Mariners' Museum, Newport News, Virginia
Maute	Paula J. Maute
National Portrait Gallery	National Portrait Gallery, Smithsonian Institution, Washington, D.C.
New-York Historical Society	New-York Historical Society, New York City
North Carolina Extension	Collection of the Humanities Extension Program at North Carolina State University, Raleigh
North Carolina Library	Thomas Wolfe Collection, Wilson Library, University of North Carolina at Chapel Hill
Pack Library	Thomas Wolfe Collection, Pack Memorial Public Library, Asheville, North Carolina
Peabody Museum	Peabody Museum of Salem, Massachusetts
Pether	Photo by Stewart Pether, by permission of Duane Schneider
Port	From the collection of Gwen Ruge Port, daughter of Edward C. Ruge
Schneider	Collection of Duane Schneider
Sisters of Providence	Sisters of Providence Archives, Seattle, Washington
Stevens Papers	James F. Stevens Papers, University of Washington Libraries, Seattle
Stites	Clara Stites
Teicher	Morton I. Teicher Collection
Wilson	Frank C. Wilson Collection

Looking Homeward

Introduction

Thomas Wolfe is one of the great writers of the twentieth century. The story of his life has become legendary and is detailed in three fine biographies and in his four autobiographical novels. In addition, his notebooks and several collections of his letters have been published, so we do not want for information about this important American literary figure.[1] Until now, however, we have not had a full photographic record of Wolfe's life. This book fills that void, drawing on many sources, not the least of which is the rich collection of photographs and snapshots made and saved by the Wolfe family. Pictures reveal character and fill in details about life experiences, and these will enhance our understanding of Wolfe's intellectual growth and development.

The photographs presented here complement the written account, which is remarkably profuse considering the brevity of Wolfe's life and of his writing career. He lived from 1900 to 1938. His first novel, *Look Homeward, Angel,*

1. Elizabeth Nowell, *Thomas Wolfe;* Andrew Turnbull, *Thomas Wolfe;* David Herbert Donald, *Look Homeward: A Life of Thomas Wolfe.* Thomas Wolfe, *Look Homeward, Angel, Of Time and the River, The Web and the Rock, You Can't Go Home Again.* Richard S. Kennedy and Paschal Reeves, eds., *The Notebooks of Thomas Wolfe;* John Skally Terry, ed., *Thomas Wolfe's Letters to His Mother;* Elizabeth Nowell, ed., *The Letters of Thomas Wolfe;* C. Hugh Holman and Sue Fields Ross, eds., *The Letters of Thomas Wolfe to His Mother;* Richard Kennedy, ed., *Beyond Love and Loyalty: The Letters of Thomas Wolfe and Elizabeth Nowell;* Suzanne Stutman, ed., *My Other Loneliness: Letters of Thomas Wolfe and Aline Bernstein* and *Holding on for Heaven: The Cables and Postcards of Thomas Wolfe and Aline Bernstein.*

was published in 1929, just nine years before his death. It was followed by *Of Time and the River* in 1935, the same year that a collection of short stories was published under the title *From Death to Morning*. There were three posthumous works—*The Web and the Rock, You Can't Go Home Again*, and *The Hills Beyond*. Numerous additional publications by and about Wolfe continue to appear. Several bibliographies list this voluminous material and attest to the indelible imprint that Wolfe left on the shape and quality of American writing and to the extent of his influence on other authors, including James Jones, Norman Mailer, Jean Stafford, James Agee, and Jack Kerouac.[2]

Wolfe grew up in Asheville, a mountain town in North Carolina that was a far cry from the picture of the South popularized by *Gone with the Wind*. That South—a land of large mansions with tall, white columns and banjo-strumming slaves who served mint juleps to their masters—was not Wolfe's South. During the early 1900s, Asheville was a middle-class town dazzled by real estate speculation, in which Wolfe's mother was an active and successful participant, much against the wishes of his father. Wolfe later referred to this buying and selling frenzy as a manifestation of grasping greed, describing that unsavory experience in harrowing detail in *You Can't Go Home Again*.

The Asheville of Wolfe's youth still suffered from the South's bitter defeat in the Civil War, from the prickly sting of poverty, and from the malignant cancer of racial injustice, prejudice, and bigotry. The middle-class nature of Asheville defined the world for Wolfe as a youngster, and it was this world that was his subject throughout his writings. Yet the optimism and boosterism of the middle class were belied for him by the poverty he saw initially in Asheville and, later, in New York during the Great Depression of the 1930s.

Wolfe's mother, Julia Westall Wolfe, was a member of a mountain clan, memorialized in his books as the "time-devouring Joyners and Pentlands." She symbolized the South for Wolfe—he always viewed the South as feminine. Julia's family was prominent in Asheville and its surroundings. Before her marriage, she was a school-

2. George R. Preston, *Thomas Wolfe: A Bibliography*; Elmer D. Johnson, *Of Time and Thomas Wolfe: A Bibliography, with a Character Index of His Works* and *Thomas Wolfe: A Checklist*; John S. Phillipson, *Thomas Wolfe: A Reference Guide*; Morton I. Teicher, "A Bibliography of Books with Selections by Thomas Wolfe"; Carol Johnston, *Thomas Wolfe: A Descriptive Bibliography*; George Garrett, *James Jones*, 50; Norman Mailer, *Advertisements for Myself*, 64; David Roberts, *Jean Stafford*, 134; Laurence Bergreen, *James Agee*, 181; Ann Charters, *Kerouac*, 133.

teacher and a book saleswoman. She met Wolfe's father—William Oliver Wolfe, a native of Pennsylvania—when she tried to sell him books, and she subsequently became his third wife. W. O., as he was known, was a stonecutter and tombstone maker who had a shop on Pack Square in Asheville. He was a vigorous man of great gusto with a crushing need to assert himself against his dreary world. He drank heavily and read widely, often quoting Shakespeare. The marriage of Wolfe's parents was unhappy, almost from the start.

In *Look Homeward, Angel* and *Of Time and the River*, Wolfe's parents appear as the characters Eliza and W. O. Gant, and his portraits of them represent some of his best writing. He visualized himself as Eugene Gant, their son, who was the fruit and fusion of two strong egos—Eliza's turned inward and W. O.'s expanding outward. While Wolfe is not often thought of as a comic writer, he wrote wonderfully humorous scenes involving W. O. as a symbol of excess, vigor, bombast, and self-pity. When W. O. decides that he has worked enough, he retires and places himself in the hands of his favorite daughter, Helen (based on Wolfe's sister Mabel). He then proceeds to bellow and rage every day instead of periodically, as had been the case while he was still working. Helen and the other children accept W. O.'s rantings as a way of life. W. O. regards his drinking as an illness that will inevitably kill him, but keeps on drinking anyhow. He curses his sickness, his family, the town of Asheville, and the world in general.

In *Look Homeward, Angel*, W. O. cries out, "Merciful God! I have fallen into the hands of fiends incarnate, more savage, more cruel, more abominable than the beasts of the field. Hell hounds that they are, they will sit by and gloat at my agony until I am done to death." One day Luke—the character based on Wolfe's brother Fred and the one son that W. O. admires because he is ambitious and has business acumen—admits that he has had an accident while driving the family car. "Jesus God!," shouts W. O. "I'm ruined." The repair bill comes to $8.92. W. O. also lectures his sons on the evils of drinking. "It would be a terrible thing if you let whiskey get the best of you. . . . You had better be dead than become a drunkard." When his son Ben—based on Wolfe's brother Ben—dies, W. O. moans, "I can't bear it. Why must you put this upon me? It'll cost me thousands of dollars before we're through burying him."

W. O. reads the obituaries every day to reinforce his belief that death, though inevitable, is for someone else—not for him. He thinks his suffering and misery are caused by others—just as in the case of Shakespeare's heros. He is convinced that his family treats him unjustly and, asserting his kinship with Julius Caesar, he thunders, "Look—in this place ran Cassius' dagger through; see what a rent the envious Casca made." Using Shakespeare's word, he knows he is not just going to die; he will "perish."

Wolfe masterfully captured W. O.'s character, and he did the same with Eliza, who was portrayed in loving satire. Wolfe's best picture of his mother is in "The Web of Earth," which was originally published in the July 1932 issue of *Scribner's Magazine* and takes up almost a hundred pages in *From Death to Morning*. Many critics feel that this is one of the finest pieces that came from Wolfe's pen. Elizabeth Nowell, Wolfe's agent and later his biographer and the editor of his letters, called it "the most perfect thing that Wolfe ever wrote." Maxwell Perkins, Wolfe's editor at Scribner's, regarded it as the "truest, the most carefully planned" of Wolfe's works. C. Hugh Holman, a Wolfe scholar who insisted that Wolfe was at his best in his short novels, ranked this one among the highest.

"The Web of Earth" is a monologue by Eliza Gant. In it she presents a vast collection of the memories, stories, and recollections that crowd her as she recalls her experiences over a period of seventy years. Wolfe described the story as weaving back and forth like a web—hence the title—and he modeled it on the portrait of Molly Bloom in James Joyce's *Ulysses,* claiming, "My old woman is a grander, richer and more tremendous figure than his was." Eliza is an earthy penny-pincher with an iron will, a mammoth memory, and a bottomless gift of gab. These traits and the strongly held prejudices that she transmitted to her children accurately characterize the wiry woman who was her real-life counterpart.

Julia's unhappiness with her husband and her growing doubts about his ability to support the family in view of his increased drinking led her to buy a boardinghouse, the Old Kentucky Home, where she moved, taking Thomas with her. W. O. and the other children remained at 92 Woodfin Street, where all eight of the Wolfe children had been born. Although the houses were just a few blocks apart, this arrangement meant that Wolfe was raised between two households. In the Old Kentucky Home, his friends were itinerant boarders, many of them drawn to the mountain climate of Asheville for treatment of their tuberculosis. Wolfe greatly admired and esteemed his brother Ben, who was his closest friend. Ben's death in the influenza epidemic of 1917 and 1918 left a scar on him that never healed. The tearfully eloquent description of Ben's dying in *Look Homeward, Angel* is powerful, emotional, and gripping.

Wolfe attended public school in Asheville until he was eleven, when he entered a new private school run by Mr.

and Mrs. J. M. Roberts—the Leonards of *Look Homeward, Angel*. A bright and perceptive student, Wolfe was almost totally absorbed in learning during his four years at the Robertses' school. Because of the small number of students there, Wolfe received personal attention, especially from Mrs. Roberts. She helped him to intensify his love of literature, an attitude instilled in him initially by his father. Wolfe later inscribed a copy of *Look Homeward, Angel* to Mrs. Roberts as "the mother of my spirit."

Shortly before reaching the age of sixteen, Wolfe entered the University of North Carolina at Chapel Hill, three years ahead of his contemporaries. The university was in the midst of a transformation from a leisurely, undergraduate liberal arts college to a major university engaged in graduate teaching and research. It subsequently became the center of southern liberalism and one of America's foremost universities. Wolfe was caught up in this change and in the opposition between the old and the new.

At Chapel Hill, after his freshman year, Wolfe was a good student and a Big Man on Campus—both literally and figuratively. He joined a fraternity and societies, wrote for school magazines and newspapers, and became the editor of the *Tar Heel*, the college newspaper. He also found much satisfaction both as an actor and as a playwright with the Carolina Playmakers under Professor Frederick Koch.

Wolfe was graduated from the University of North Carolina at the age of twenty, eager to study further in order to become a playwright. He went to Harvard, where he remained for three years, earning a Master of Arts degree in literature. He completed the degree requirements in two years but remained for another year in order to do more work under Professor George Pierce Baker in his 47 Workshop, a program designed to prepare students for the theater. Baker's students included Phillip Barry, John Mason Brown, Eugene O'Neill, Sidney Howard, S. N. Behrman, Elia Kazan, and Van Wyck Brooks. *Of Time and the River* contains a satiric picture of the 47 Workshop, attacking its pretentiousness.

A few professors at Harvard praised Wolfe's ability as a scholar and urged him to go on to a Ph.D. and a career in academia. However, Wolfe was determined to be a playwright. He tried vainly to market his plays in New York. *Welcome to Our City*, which had been produced by the 47 Workshop, was considered for several months by the Theatre Guild but finally rejected. Wolfe reluctantly acknowledged that he was going no place in the theater, and he took a job as an English instructor at New York University in February 1924.

Wolfe taught at New York University off and on from 1924 until 1930. In *Of Time and the River*, he lampoons it as the "School of Utility Cultures." During this period, Wolfe made several trips to Europe, trying to fulfill a wanderlust that started when he was a child. At the end of his first trip, he met Aline Bernstein, a successful set and costume designer in the New York theater world, and they began a passionate love affair. She was eighteen years his senior, married, and the mother of two children. Mrs. Bernstein is the Esther Jack of the later novels and the A. B. to whom *Look Homeward, Angel* is dedicated. She recounted their romance in *Three Blue Suits* and *The Journey Down*. She also wrote an autobiography, *An Actor's Daughter*, in which she lovingly described her father, Joseph Frankau.

In June 1926, while in England, Wolfe began to put down in large ledgers, which Mrs. Bernstein bought for him, the accelerating flood of his childhood memories. The mounting pages of manuscript had many literary references that showed the deep immersion in literature that characterized Wolfe's life up to that point. The writing, according to Wolfe himself, bore the mark of James Joyce's *Ulysses*. In addition, the influence of Sinclair Lewis is discernible in *Look Homeward, Angel*.

When Wolfe returned to New York in December 1926, he continued to work on his manuscript, then called *O Lost*, as his love affair with Aline Bernstein ran its tempestuous course. She undoubtedly assisted him in curbing his monumental flow of words and his enormous output of energy. Just how much she helped to shape *Look Homeward, Angel* is a matter for debate, but she surely exercised some influence in disciplining Wolfe's writing. Wolfe recognized her artistic, emotional, and financial support when he dedicated the book to her.

The work was finally completed in March 1928, and Wolfe sailed for Europe again on June 30. He left the manuscript with Madeline Boyd, a literary agent to whom Mrs. Bernstein had introduced him. Wolfe returned to New York on December 31, 1928, and found a letter from Maxwell Perkins of Charles Scribner's Sons expressing interest in acquiring the book—"if it could be worked into a form publishable by us."

Wolfe renewed his affair with Mrs. Bernstein and struggled desperately, with considerable help from Perkins, to shorten the manuscript in order to make it acceptable to Scribner's. The book was finally published in October 1929, the month of the stock market crash preceding the Great Depression of the 1930s. It was hardly an auspicious time for the appearance of a first novel by an unknown author.

As first submitted by Wolfe, *Look Homeward, Angel* was

the detailed, intense record of the ancestry, birth, child-hood, and youth of Eugene Gant. It began with a ninety-page sequence on the life of Eugene's father, and it ended with an imaginary conversation with the ghost of Ben in which Eugene discovers that "you are your world." This final scene took place after Eugene's graduation from col-lege as he left home, turning his eyes to the distant, soar-ing mountain ranges. Perkins insisted on the deletion of the historical opening as well as the removal of other ma-terial that he considered extraneous. He also recom-mended several rearrangements. Perkins has been charged with having excessive influence, and this was later a fac-tor in Wolfe's break with Scribner's. However, most crit-ics agree that the manuscript received no more editing than is customary for the works of exuberant first nov-elists.

In fact, *Look Homeward, Angel* is much more Wolfe's in writing and execution than any other work published under his name. Its lyric intensity and its dramatic power were immediately acknowledged and hailed. Wolfe quickly became recognized as a figure to be reckoned with in the literary world. He was given a boost by Sinclair Lewis, who praised Wolfe in his 1930 Nobel Prize acceptance speech. A career of great promise was launched with the publication of *Look Homeward, Angel*.

In the midst of the praise the book received, a discor-dant note arose from Asheville, which was collectively in-dignant. The residents there did not like the portrait of themselves and their town that they saw in the book. Members of Wolfe's family were hurt, and the people of Asheville were angry, causing Wolfe, who had hungered for fame, to decide that he really didn't want it. Moreover, he was weighed down by the pressure to produce a sec-ond book that would fulfill the promise of the first. This became one of the major struggles of his life.

Wolfe resigned from New York University early in 1930, ended the affair with Mrs. Bernstein, and went to Europe on a Guggenheim fellowship. When he returned to America in February 1931 after nine months of wan-dering through Europe, he established himself in a base-ment apartment in Brooklyn where he wrestled with his writing, as described factually in *The Story of a Novel* and fictionally in *You Can't Go Home Again*.

Even before *Look Homeward, Angel* was published, Wolfe had begun planning the new book and writing parts of it. During those lonely years in Brooklyn, he labored desper-ately to produce the second book. In 1932, his story "Por-trait of Bascom Hawke" shared the *Scribner's Magazine* prize for the best short story of the year and netted Wolfe $2,500, half the prize money. He published several other short stories during this period from 1931 to 1935. Though he was barely subsisting on the slender proceeds of these magazine publications, when he was approached by Metro-Goldwyn-Mayer about the possibility of writing movie scripts for $1,000 to $1,500 a week, he said no on the grounds that he had a lot of books to write. A few years later, when Wolfe visited Hollywood, the offer was renewed but just as firmly rejected. That occasion was described in a pamphlet by Samuel Marx, who wrote that Wolfe was asked as part of Hollywood's effort to woo him whether he would like to meet any movie stars. According to the story, Wolfe named Jean Harlow, and they hit it off so well that she took him home. He left Hollywood the next morning.[3]

The novel Wolfe worked on in Brooklyn from 1931 to 1935 was a vast work originally called *The October Fair*. It was to be in four volumes and extend in time from the Civil War to the present. There were to be hundreds of characters and a new protagonist named David Hawke to replace Eugene Gant. Perkins worked closely with Wolfe to give the work an acceptable structure. Although Perkins himself left no records to help us understand his role, Wolfe wrote extensively about Perkins's significant contribution in letters, in notebooks, and, eventually, in *The*

3. Samuel Marx, *Thomas Wolfe and Hollywood*.

Story of a Novel. Perkins convinced Wolfe to omit his rhapsodic vision of America and to concentrate on writing an autobiographical novel. He persuaded Wolfe to abandon David Hawke and return to Eugene Gant. The theme of the search for a father was suggested by Perkins, and he helped Wolfe to work out the structure of what became *Of Time and the River*. At long last, Perkins sent the manuscript to the printer, even though Wolfe protested that it required further work.

Of Time and the River is a gargantuan book—almost a thousand pages. It continues the saga of Eugene Gant's life. The story opens as Eugene leaves Altamont for Harvard; it follows him there and then to New York, where he teaches at the "School of Utility Cultures." His first trip to Europe is narrated, including his frustrating affair with Ann, who is in love with the homosexual Francis Starwick, Wolfe's fictional version of Kenneth Raisbeck, Professor Baker's assistant in the 47 Workshop. The book concludes as Eugene meets a woman named Esther on the ship taking him home to the United States.

Look Homeward, Angel and *Of Time and the River* are linked in the sense that the second book may be called a sequel to the first. However, there are acute differences between the two. *Look Homeward, Angel* is unified in its focus on one family, a mountain town, and a way of life.

It recounts the keen impressions of youth, leading inexorably to the moment of self-awareness that ends the book. By contrast, *Of Time and the River* has less plot and more soul-searching. Some sections of the book have little relevance to its theme, so that structural cohesion is lacking. The best scenes and the most effective portraits sometimes seem to be dramatic intrusions. Yet Wolfe's rhetoric in *Of Time and the River* is often wonderful, and poetic passages abound. The novel has some of Wolfe's best writing—and some of his worst.

Reactions to *Of Time and the River* were mixed. Many reviewers hailed it as fulfilling the promise Wolfe had shown in *Look Homeward, Angel*. Others found fault with its formlessness, its dearth of plot, and its euphoric extravagances. The questions that have subsequently been debated about Wolfe's work were first formulated as critics looked at *Of Time and the River*. Is it legitimate in fiction to substitute reporting and autobiography for genuine creation? How much help should an author get from his editor? What constitutes acceptable form? Despite the critics' many reservations, *Of Time and the River* became a best-seller, and some commentators called Wolfe a worthy successor to Melville and Whitman. They held that his first two novels demonstrated his capacity to produce the great American novel—in the future.

In the fall of 1935, fourteen selections excluded from *Of Time and the River*—some of them previously published in magazines—were assembled into *From Death to Morning*. The stories in this collection are uneven in quality, but they show Wolfe as a serious experimenter in fiction. His mastery of the short story is demonstrated in "Only the Dead Know Brooklyn," "In the Park," and "Death the Proud Brother." While these stories show Wolfe's technical skill, they also provide additional evidence of his reliance on his own life experiences in his work. This led one reviewer to say, "The present collection has its brilliant moments, but the total effect of the book is to make one uneasy about Mr. Wolfe's future development as an artist." On the other hand, another critic described the anthology as surging "with the ebullience of his original if untidy prose."[4]

Wolfe's wanderlust led him to make seven trips to Europe in the twelve years from 1924 to 1936. He traveled to Berlin in 1935 and 1936, slowly becoming disenchanted with the Germans, whom he had previously admired. He saw through the mask of Nazism to the terrible things behind it, and he wrote a poignant story called "I Have a

4. Howard Mumford Jones, "Thomas Wolfe's Short Stories"; Rollene W. Saal, "Pick of the Paperbacks."

Thing to Tell You" that showed sympathetic understanding of the plight of Jews under the Nazis. His sensitivity and his budding liberal viewpoint were remarkable given the provincialism and anti-Semitism he had manifested earlier.

In 1936, Wolfe published *The Story of a Novel*. Based on a lecture he gave at a writers' conference in Colorado, it describes with humility and honesty how he wrote *Of Time and the River*. The revelations proved to some critics that Wolfe was not a novelist but rather an autobiographer. A further accusation was that Wolfe wrote entirely under the direction of Maxwell Perkins. The most savage attack came from Bernard DeVoto, who reviewed *The Story of a Novel* in the *Saturday Review of Literature*. Beginning by complimenting Wolfe for his truthfulness, DeVoto went on to call Wolfe "infantile" and "immature." He said, "However useful genius may be in the writing of novels, it is not enough in itself—it never has been enough in any art. . . . Until Mr. Wolfe develops more craftsmanship, he will not be the important novelist he is now widely accepted as being." DeVoto called his article "Genius Is Not Enough."

DeVoto's devastating broadside hurt Wolfe deeply and helped him decide to change publishers in order to show that he was not dependent on Perkins. He had some other concerns as well. Perkins's consistently conservative political views were at marked variance with Wolfe's increasingly liberal outlook. Also, Wolfe was dissatisfied with the way Scribner's had handled a lawsuit brought by Madeline Boyd to collect a commission on the royalties from *Of Time and the River*. The agonizing break with Scribner's began in mid–1936 and was completed at the end of 1937, when Wolfe signed a contract with Harper and Brothers. Edward C. Aswell replaced Perkins as his editor. The relationship between Wolfe and Aswell, although short-lived, was very close for the few months before Wolfe's death; he spent his last Christmas at the Aswell home in Chappaqua, New York.

In the summer of 1937, Wolfe worked in a cabin at Oteen, near Asheville. It was his first trip home since the publication of *Look Homeward, Angel*. The people of Asheville who had reviled Wolfe were now ready to receive him with pride. Wolfe welcomed the warm reception, but he decided that "you can't go home again"—he had to move onward, not backward.

Despite many interruptions by admirers who wanted to meet him, Wolfe did some writing in Oteen, which he continued during the rest of the year and in the first few months of 1938. He was back to the notion of a four-volume magnum opus that he perceived as the tale of an innocent man's discovery of life and the world. He gave the name George Webber to his protagonist, and he portrayed him as physically similar to David Hawke, the character he had wanted to use earlier as a replacement for Eugene Gant.

In May 1938, Wolfe turned over to Aswell two enormous bundles of manuscript, placing the rest in a crate destined for storage. He then left on a tour of the West that ended when he became seriously ill in Seattle. When his condition worsened, he was taken to Johns Hopkins Hospital in Baltimore. He died there on September 15, 1938, just eighteen days before his thirty-eighth birthday.

Aswell extracted three books from the mountain of manuscript that Wolfe had left with him before his last trip. The first was *The Web and the Rock*, published in 1939. This book appears to be similar to the one that Wolfe had planned as the initiator of the four-volume series. Four hundred pages of *The Web and the Rock* have the exuberant and extravagant style found in *Of Time and the River*. However, the opening sections, prepared for publication during the final years of Wolfe's life, are sparser rhetorically and show more control over the material. Although *The Web and the Rock* forces two disparate parts together, it is more of a novel than *Of Time and the River* in that it begins, develops, and ends. The protagonist, George Webber, is clearly based on Wolfe, as was Eugene Gant, but his physical characteristics and his family life have changed.

The Web and the Rock expresses Wolfe's determination to read all the books, see all the sights, eat all the food, love all the women, and know all the men in the world. It discloses his insatiable lust of belly, heart, and brain. Up to the beginning of George Webber's romance with Esther Jack, the story in *The Web and the Rock* is similar to that in the first two novels. A country boy is born and educated. The web of life in a provincial town spins around him, as symbolized by his name, Webber. He carries the web with him to the rock of New York, where he teaches, writes, and begins his journeys, consumed by a hunger he cannot satisfy.

The romance between Webber and Esther Jack joins two people who are antitheses of each other. She is beautiful; he is plain. She belongs to the city; he, to the country. She is an artist in small things; he, in large. She is close to middle age; he is in his twenties. She is Jewish; he is Gentile. She is bright and gregarious; he is dark and lonely. The web of their love envelops them and enables Webber to resolve the hunger that tortured him for ten years. At the end of the book, Esther is in New York and Webber in Germany, where he discovers the flaw in his philosophy. Instead of trying to remember eight million faces, to read two million books, to love all women, it is better to re-member one face, to write one wise book, to love one woman. *The Web and the Rock* has brilliance, vitality, ener-gy, and power. It shows Wolfe's gifts for satire and humor. Many passages deserve to be read aloud.

The second book Aswell put together was published in 1940 under the title *You Can't Go Home Again.*[5] It is much less of a novel than *The Web and the Rock,* presenting large units of material that Wolfe had completed but only par-tially arranged at the time of his death. Aswell organized them to form the loosely structured narrative of Webber's life after he returns from the trip to Germany that con-cludes *The Web and the Rock.* Webber goes to his home-town to attend his aunt's funeral and then travels again to Europe, where he meets Lloyd McHarg—based on Sin-clair Lewis. He visits Germany, where he comprehends the horror of the Nazi regime and, finally, writes a long letter to Foxhall Edwards—Maxwell Perkins—in which he sets forth his credo. These last two sections of the book contain some of Wolfe's most forceful writing.

5. Wolfe first heard this often-quoted phrase of his from Ella Winter, the widow of Lincoln Steffens. In her autobiography *And Not to Yield* she de-scribed the incident in which she spoke the words (176–77). Wolfe reacted enthusiastically and asked her permission to use them.

The individual scenes in *You Can't Go Home Again* dem-onstrate Wolfe's capacity to bring his characters to life. However, as a collection of disjointed particles, it is prob-ably the least satisfactory of Wolfe's novels. At the same time, it shows Wolfe as a social critic. The Russians, who detected Marxist tendencies in the book, had it translated into Russian. A better description of Wolfe's politics would be that he became a southern populist with some remain-ing tinges of southern conservatism. The FBI apparently had suspicions about Wolfe, since it maintained a file on him. Yet the heavily censored version of the file available under the Freedom of Information Act shows no evidence of left-wing affiliations.[6] This conclusion is substantiated by the patriotic declaration of faith in the promise of America that is to be found in *You Can't Go Home Again,* which Wolfe ended with a triumphant affirmation of the American ideals of freedom and equality.

The third volume that Aswell mined from the manu-script left by Wolfe was *The Hills Beyond,* a collection of seven short stories, some of which had appeared previ-ously in magazines, a one-act play, two essays, and the fifty-thousand-word novel that gives the book its title. In

6. Herbert Mitgang, *Dangerous Dossiers,* 99–101.

addition, *The Hills Beyond* contains "A Note on Thomas Wolfe," in which Aswell explains Wolfe's writing habits and describes the "mountain of manuscript" that Wolfe left with him. Several of the stories in this collection are outstanding. "Chickamauga" is a first-person Civil War reminiscence based on the stories of Wolfe's great-uncle. It is a potent study of frustration, complete in itself—unlike most of his other writings, which he saw as parts of longer works. "The Lost Boy" tells about the death of Wolfe's brother Grover at the St. Louis World's Fair of 1904. Another fine autobiographical piece, "God's Lonely Man," gives further evidence of Wolfe's preoccupation with the theme of loneliness.

Before putting these three books together, Aswell talked with Elizabeth Nowell, Wolfe's agent, and with Maxwell Perkins, his editor at Scribner's, to learn more about Wolfe's intentions. He then undertook a cut-and-paste job that resulted in his having a large hand in the structure of the posthumous publications. Some critics claimed that he exceeded the responsibilities of an editor, but two leading Wolfe scholars, Richard Kennedy and Leslie Field, have asserted that Aswell's contribution was both necessary and appropriate.[7]

The measure of Wolfe's achievement is large indeed.

His work is peopled with a host of vibrant characters, and some of his best writing is truly magnificent. His vast vocabulary, his rousing rhetoric, his luminous lyricism, and his expressive eloquence are unmatched in American prose. His best work communicates his delight in the shapes, sounds, colors, odors, and textures of experience. He had a nostalgia for things past, and he set down his impressions with total authority.

Of course, passages of bad writing and irrelevant action are sprinkled throughout Wolfe's books. But persistently present in his work are the perceptive insights of a man who tried to portray America, using language as rich, as beautiful, and as opulent as America itself. At his best, Wolfe could make words do magical things—caress, stir, state, burst, and explode. He did this without economy of phrase, depending on torrential overflows of adjectives and adverbs. He had abundant imaginative power and passion—so much so that he often said too much. This was not the frailty of a weak writer. It was the fragility of a strong writer—perhaps one of America's finest novelists.

During his altogether too short life, Wolfe moved from

7. Richard Kennedy, "The Wolfegate Affair"; Leslie Field, *Thomas Wolfe and His Editors.*

being a provincial southerner to becoming an incisive social critic who might have written some great social novels. His hope for the world and for the future is best expressed in the last chapter of *You Can't Go Home Again* where, in George Webber's final letter to Foxhall Edwards, Wolfe expressed the basic difference between his fundamentally optimistic stance and Perkins's essentially fatalistic view. Wolfe's ultimate belief is stated in the following memorable lines: "Man was born to live, to suffer and to die and what befalls him is a tragic lot. There is no denying this in the final end. But, we must, dear Fox, deny it all along the way."

1. Birth

Thomas Wolfe was born in Asheville—a small mountain town in western North Carolina—on October 3, 1900, as duly recorded in the family Bible. His birthplace was the family home at 92 Woodfin Street.

Pack Library

In his fiction, Wolfe referred to Asheville first as "Altamont" and, later, as "Libya Hill." In **Look Homeward, Angel**, he described it as "sprawled out on its hundred hills and hollows."

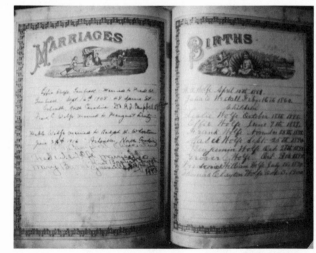

The family Bible listed the birth dates of Wolfe, his parents, and his siblings. It also registered the marriages of Wolfe's sisters Effie and Mabel and of his brothers Frank and Fred.

Pack Library

Pack Library

The house in which the Wolfe children were born was built by their father, William Oliver Wolfe, who also planted a garden with flowers, trees, and vines and who paved the walk with marble. In **Look Homeward, Angel**, Wolfe wrote that for W. O. Gant, the fictional counterpart of his father, "the house was the picture of his soul, the garment of his will." This sketch was drawn by Walter E. Bearden, July 7, 1917.

Brewer

William Oliver Wolfe built the medallion bed in which all the Wolfe children were born. It was later moved to the Old Kentucky Home, which Wolfe's mother, Julia Westall Wolfe, bought as a boarding-house in 1906.

Pack Library

On July 4, 1899, fifteen months before Thomas Wolfe was born, a family portrait was taken in front of 92 Woodfin Street. Left to right: Effie, William Oliver Wolfe, Mabel, Fred, Grover, Ben, Julia Wolfe, and Frank.

Pack Library

The birthplace of Thomas Wolfe at 92 Woodfin Street as it looked in 1935 just before it was torn down.

In 1990, to commemorate the ninetieth anniversary of Wolfe's birth, a marker was placed in the parking lot of the Asheville YMCA to indicate where the house in which the Wolfe children were born had stood. The house, a victim of neglect and decay, had been razed when Asheville was redeveloped. Part of the site is now occupied by an expressway and part by the YMCA.

Teicher

2. Parents

Julia Westall Wolfe, Thomas's mother, came from a large family that was prominent in the Asheville area. His father, William Oliver Wolfe, a native of Pennsylvania, was a stonecutter and tombstone maker. He was divorced from his first wife, and his second wife had died. He married Julia after a chance meeting when Julia tried to sell him some books. The marriage was an unhappy one; it proved to Thomas that life was a mystery, dependent on accidents of fate.

Pack Library

Julia Westall and William Oliver Wolfe were married on January 14, 1885. In **Look Homeward, Angel**, Thomas Wolfe called the characters based on his parents Eliza and W. O. Gant, and he designated May as the month for their wedding.

*In **Look Homeward, Angel**, when W. O. Gant first meets Eliza, he thinks, "She's a pippin as sure as you're born." Julia, on whom the character of Eliza was based, is shown here at the age of twenty-four, a year before she was married.*

Julia Westall Wolfe in 1944.

Julia Wolfe holding a picture of Thomas as an infant.

Braden-Hatchett

Julia Wolfe's gnarled hands holding
one of her many letters from Thomas.
The letters were edited by John Skally
Terry and published in 1943 with many
errors. A corrected edition, edited by
C. Hugh Holman and Sue Fields Ross,
was published in 1968.

Pack Library

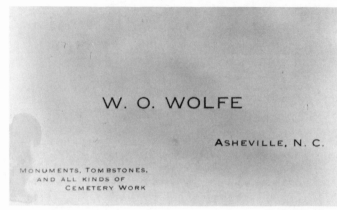

W. O. WOLFE

ASHEVILLE, N. C.

MONUMENTS, TOMBSTONES,
AND ALL KINDS OF
CEMETERY WORK

W. O. Wolfe's business card.

William Oliver Wolfe lived from 1851 to 1922. He died in Johns Hopkins Hospital, Baltimore, where Wolfe himself was to die sixteen years later.

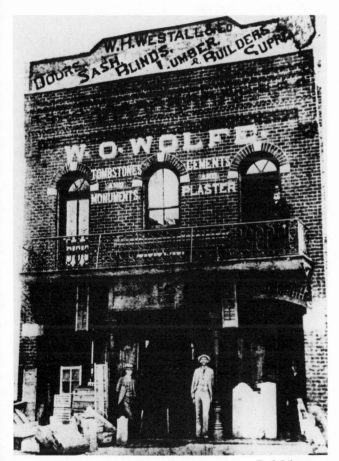

W. O. Wolfe's tombstone shop was at 28 Pack Square in Asheville. It was built by him on property that Julia Wolfe had purchased shortly before they were married. The Jackson Building now stands on the site.

This angel, which W. O. Wolfe sold from his shop and which Thomas Wolfe described in **Look Homeward, Angel** as having been purchased by "Queen" Elizabeth to stand over the grave of one of her prostitutes, is now located in Oakdale Cemetery, Hendersonville, North Carolina, twenty-two miles south of Asheville.

Pack Library

Magi

3. Siblings

Wolfe's older brothers and sisters were: Leslie, 1885–1886; Effie, 1887–1950; Frank, 1888–1956; Mabel, 1890–1958; Grover, 1892–1904; Ben, 1892–1918; and Fred, 1894–1980. In *Look Homeward, Angel*, Leslie is referred to only as an infant daughter of Eliza's. Effie is called Daisy Gant. Frank is called Steve Gant. Mabel is called Helen, and her married name is Barton. The characters based on Grover and Ben have the same first names as Thomas's brothers, with their last name changed to Gant. Fred is called Luke Gant.

Leslie, the firstborn child of Julia and William Oliver Wolfe, died of cholera in 1886 when she was nine months old. She is shown here with her mother.

By 1897, the Wolfes had six living children. They appear here with their mother on March 21, during a visit to St. Augustine, Florida. Left to right: Frank, Julia, Fred in front of Mabel, Effie, Ben, and Grover.

Effie at the age of eighteen. She married Fred C. Gambrell in 1908 and moved to South Carolina.

Pack Library

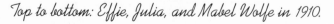

Top to bottom: Effie, Julia, and Mabel Wolfe in 1910.

Pack Library

Pack Library

Frank in 1906 at the age of nineteen.

Frank on a visit to Chicago in 1914 at the age of twenty-six.

Pack Library

Pack Library

Mabel Wolfe in 1915 at the age of twenty-five.

Pack Library

*Ben, Thomas Wolfe's favorite brother, in his early teens. The description in **Look Homeward, Angel** of Ben's death during the influenza epidemic of 1917–1918 is one of the finest passages written by Wolfe.*

Pack Library

Ben in 1915 at the age of twenty-three.

Grover, Ben's twin, died of typhoid fever in St. Louis on November 16, 1904, at the age of twelve.

A family portrait taken in front of 92 Woodfin Street in 1915. At the far left, from left to right, are Thomas, Julia, and W. O. Wolfe. At the far right, from right to left, are Ben, Mabel, and Fred. The others are unidentified.

Mabel married Ralph Wheaton on June 28, 1916. The wedding party, from left to right, consisted of: Eugenia Brown; Thomas; Thelma Osborne; Mrs. C. A. Wheaton, mother of the groom; Miriam Gambrell, flower girl; Mrs. Geraldine Norton, sister of the groom; Fred; Pearl Shope; Ralph Wheaton; Mabel; Effie; Ben; Sarah Lee Brown, flower girl; Julia; W. O.; Claudia Osborne; and Fred C. Gambrell, Effie's husband.

Pack Library

Mabel and Ralph Wheaton in 1918. In **Look Homeward, Angel,** *they are called Helen and Hugh Barton.*

Pack Library

Fred was Thomas Wolfe's last surviving sibling. He devoted the final years of his life to memorializing his brother, often introducing himself as Luke, his fictional counterpart in **Look Homeward, Angel**. This photograph shows Fred when he was a student at Georgia Tech in 1914–1915.

Fred and Julia Wolfe in front of the Old Kentucky Home in 1920.

Fred Wolfe in 1958.

4. Early Years, 1900–1904

For several years after Thomas was born, his mother continued to regard him as her infant. He slept in her bed, and she looked after him as though he remained a baby. In 1904, she took all seven children to St. Louis, where she ran a boardinghouse at the World's Fair. The trip turned out tragically when Grover died of typhoid fever. Wolfe wrote about this sad experience in one of his best short stories, "The Lost Boy," originally published in *Redbook Magazine* and later reprinted in *The Hills Beyond*.

North Carolina Library

Thomas Wolfe at the age of nine months.

Thomas Wolfe at the age of four.

Another view of Thomas Wolfe at the age of four.

Thomas Wolfe at the age of three.

Braden-Hatchett

The North Carolina, Julia Wolfe's boardinghouse in St. Louis during the 1904 World's Fair, was located at 5095 Fairmount Avenue. In this photograph Fred Wolfe is standing in the doorway. The men sitting on the steps are North Carolinians on a visit to the fair.

Pack Library

Frank Wolfe's photograph on his pass to the St. Louis World's Fair.

5. Childhood and Youth, 1906–1915

Thomas Wolfe's elementary and secondary education took place at the Orange Street Public School and the North State Fitting School. He quickly learned to read, played with classmates, sold the *Saturday Evening Post*, attended Sunday school, delivered newspapers, and traveled with his mother to Florida, Arkansas, and New Orleans. Lifelong habits of voracious reading and restless traveling were instilled at an early age.

Pack Library

Thomas Wolfe began his education in September 1906 at the Orange Street School, where he was accepted even though he was one month short of the required age of six. The building was opened in 1888, condemned in 1939, and later destroyed; this photograph was taken in 1904.

Elizabeth Bernard Hester, Thomas Wolfe's first-grade teacher.

Pack Library

North Carolina Library

Thomas Wolfe at seven, a year after he started school.

Pack Library

Thomas Wolfe at the age of eight, with his cousin Mary Louise Wolfe. The picture was taken on Sunday, February 21, 1909, and shows how old Thomas was before his mother agreed to cut his curls.

Pack Library

The Orange Street fifth grade class in 1910. Thomas Wolfe is seated at the left end of the front row. The teacher, Bessie Moody, is standing at left end of the third row.

North Carolina Library

Pack Library

The North State Fitting School was a private school that had just opened when Thomas Wolfe became its first student in 1912.

Thomas Wolfe at eleven.

Margaret Roberts, the wife of J. M. Roberts and a teacher at the North State Fitting School, fostered Wolfe's love of literature and nurtured his desire to become a writer.

Pack Library

Wolfe inscribed one of the first copies of **Look Homeward, Angel** to Margaret Roberts, calling her "the mother of my spirit."

Look Homeward, Angel

A Story of the Buried Life

BY

THOMAS WOLFE

"At one time the earth was probably a white-hot sphere like the sun."
—TARR AND McMURRY

To Margaret Roberts,
who was the mother of my spirit,
I present this copy of my first book,
with love and with devotion

Thomas Wolfe
Oct 15, 1929

CHARLES SCRIBNER'S SONS
NEW YORK
1929

Pack Library

Mr. and Mrs. J. M. Roberts, their son, Buddy, and their daughter, Margaret.

J. M. Roberts, founder of the North State Fitting School, at the age of seventy-eight, sitting in the parlor of the Old Kentucky Home.

North Carolina Library

Thomas Wolfe at the age of thirteen.

For two years, beginning at the age of fourteen, Thomas Wolfe had a paper route that included Valley Street, the area shown in this photograph

Pack Library

North Carolina Library

Thomas Wolfe at the age of fifteen.

Pack Library

Students of the North State Fitting School in 1915. Left to right: Henry Harris, Thomas Wolfe, Joe Taylor, Julius Martin, Junius Horner, Reid Russell, and Fred Thomas.

6. The Old Kentucky Home

On August 30, 1906, Julia Wolfe bought the Old Kentucky Home, a large house at 48 Spruce Street in Asheville. She opened it as a boardinghouse, catering to guests looking for a vacation resort or to those coming to the mountains to be treated for tuberculosis. She moved there herself, taking Thomas with her, while her husband and the other children remained in the house on Woodfin Street. Since the two houses were only a few blocks apart, they all visited back and forth frequently. In *Look Homeward, Angel,* the Old Kentucky Home is called Dixieland.

TELEPHONE 4449 W   REASONABLE RATES

OLD KENTUCKY HOME
ONE BLOCK NORTH OF COURT HOUSE

JULIA E. WOLFE   48 SPRUCE ST.
PROP.   ASHEVILLE, N. C.

Magi

The Old Kentucky Home card.

Pack Library

The Old Kentucky Home shortly after it was purchased by Julia Wolfe. She is sitting on the porch, W. O. and Mabel are on the lawn, and Thomas is in the right foreground. The boy on the side porch behind W. O. may be Ben.

Another view of the Old Kentucky Home.

Gordon

Brewer

The porch of the Old Kentucky Home. In **Look Homeward, Angel**, this is where Eugene Gant courted Laura
James, a boarder.

Pack Library

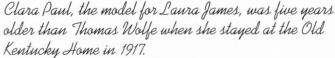

Clara Paul, the model for Laura James, was five years
older than Thomas Wolfe when she stayed at the Old
Kentucky Home in 1917.

Brewer

Brewer

The porch where Eugene slept during the summer of his first love.

The windows to the second-story porch face the windows of the adjacent bedroom where Laura James slept. Eugene climbed through these windows to visit Laura in secret.

Brewer

The bedroom where Eugene and Laura made love.

Brewer

In declining health, William Oliver Wolfe spent the last years of his life in this bedroom at the Old Kentucky Home.

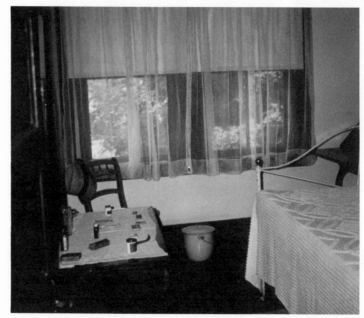

Brewer

Julia Wolfe slept in this small bedroom near the kitchen in order to have better access to the downstairs activities of the boardinghouse.

*The bedroom in which Ben died in 1918. In **Look Homeward, Angel**, Wolfe wrote, "We can believe in the nothingness of life, we can believe in the nothingness of death and of life after death but who can believe in the nothingness of Ben?"*

Brewer

Brewer

The kitchen of the Old Kentucky Home, where Julia Wolfe prepared sumptuous meals to satisfy the appetites of her boarders.

The kitchen area where Mabel pressed linens for the dining room.

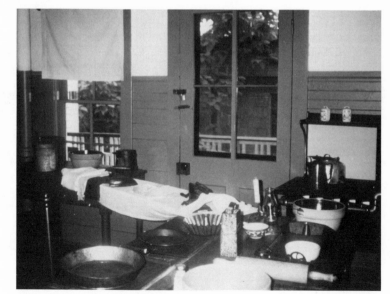

Brewer

Brewer

The dining room, where Julia Wolfe served as many as fifty boarders at a time.

Brewer

The parlor, where Mabel would play the piano and where W. O. Wolfe would build roaring fires on cold mornings.

Thomas Wolfe with a group of boarders on the side lawn of the Old Kentucky Home in 1915. The woman sitting directly in front of Wolfe was Mrs. Clarence Trim; the others are unidentified.

Pack Library

Pack Library

The train depot where Thomas Wolfe would pass out cards trying to attract boarders to the Old Kentucky Home.

Teicher

The Old Kentucky Home is now the Thomas Wolfe Memorial.

Teicher

The entrance hall to the Thomas Wolfe Memorial is filled with Wolfe memorabilia.

Brewer

An assortment of tools from W. O. Wolfe's tombstone shop is displayed in the Thomas Wolfe Memorial.

Some of Thomas Wolfe's clothing, brought from New York, hangs in a closet in the Thomas Wolfe Memorial.

Brewer

Brewer

One of the old boardinghouse guest rooms now houses Thomas Wolfe's possessions, brought from his New York apartment by his brother Fred.

7. The University of North Carolina at Chapel Hill, 1916–1920

In 1916, shortly before reaching the age of sixteen, Thomas Wolfe enrolled at the University of North Carolina at Chapel Hill. The buildings in which he lived, studied, ate, and worked included Old East, New West, Swain Hall, Alumni Hall, and the YMCA. During his years at the university he was strongly influenced by several professors who are described in *Look Homeward, Angel*. He was also active in extracurricular activities, editing the school newspaper, writing and acting in plays, joining various student organizations, including a fraternity, and generally becoming a Big Man on Campus. His biography in *Yakety-Yak*, the yearbook for 1920, the year he graduated, called him a "young Shakespeare" and said, "It is no wonder that he is classed as a genius."

Thomas Wolfe in 1916, the year he entered the University of North Carolina.

North Carolina Library

Teicher

The Old Well is the symbol of the University of North Carolina.

Old East, dating back to 1793, was the first state university building in the United States. A dormitory today, it was a classroom building in which Wolfe studied when he was at Chapel Hill.

Teicher

While at the University of North Carolina, Wolfe was a member of the Dialectic Society, one of two literary societies whose purpose was to train students for debate and public speaking. The Dialectic and Philanthropic societies have since merged to form the Di-Phi Society, which meets on the third floor of New West.

Teicher

*From **Yakety-Yak**, the University of North Carolina yearbook, 1918.*

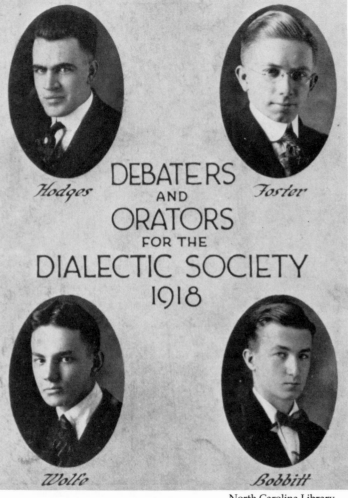

Teicher

A portrait of Wolfe hangs in the Di-Phi Room in New West. It is a tradition for the literary societies to hang portraits in their chambers of members who have made names for themselves statewide and nationally. As a student, Wolfe brashly, but presciently, said that his portrait would hang there one day.

Teicher

Swain Hall, the college commons, where Wolfe ate many of his meals. In **Look Homeward, Angel**, he calls it Stiggins Hall and says that students referred to it as "The Sty." Actually, they called Swain Hall "Swine Hall."

Teicher

The YMCA, where Wolfe edited the **Tar Heel**, the campus newspaper.

Alumni Hall, where Wolfe attended classes.

Teicher

North Carolina Library

*During his junior and senior years, Wolfe took courses from Horace Williams, professor of philosophy. Along with Margaret Roberts and Edwin Greenlaw, Wolfe considered Williams to be one of the great teachers he had encountered. In **Look Homeward, Angel**, Williams is called Virgil Weldon.*

North Carolina Library

Wolfe studied with William Stanly "Bully" Bernard, professor of Greek, during his freshman and sophomore years, acquiring a lasting appreciation for the Greek language. In **Look Homeward, Angel**, Bernard is Edward Pettigrew "Buck" Benson.

North Carolina Library

For three of his four years at Chapel Hill, Wolfe studied English literature, English composition, and the English Renaissance with Edwin Greenlaw, professor of English. On one occasion, Wolfe wrote an essay for him on toilet paper, claiming that was all he could find. After hearing Wolfe read a few paragraphs, Greenlaw asserted that the essay was written on the right kind of paper.

Teicher

As a junior and senior, Wolfe took courses in Shakespeare and playwriting from Frederick H. Koch, professor of drama. Koch was the organizer of the Carolina Playmakers, a group that presented student plays. The Playmakers staged two of Wolfe's plays, and Koch urged Wolfe to continue studying drama under Professor George Pierce Baker at Harvard. In **Look Homeward, Angel**, Koch is George C. Rockham.

North Carolina Library

*Wolfe in the title role of his play **The Return of Buck Gavin**, presented by the Carolina Playmakers on March 14–15, 1919.*

*A scene from Wolfe's play **The Third Night**, presented by the Carolina Playmakers on December 12, 1919. The actors are Jonathan Daniels (sitting), Frederick J. Cohn (standing behind him), and Wolfe.*

North Carolina Library

Wolfe at Chapel Hill in 1918.

ASHEVILLE BOY SCORES SUCCESS AT UNIVERSITY

Play Written By Thomas C. Wolfe, of This City, Makes Big Hit

Pack Library

From the Asheville Citizen.

North Carolina Library

Wolfe and fellow student E. A. Griffen, Chapel Hill, 1918.

Wolfe (center) on the porch of the Pi Kappa Phi fraternity house in Chapel Hill in the spring of 1919.

North Carolina Library

North Carolina Library

Wolfe, standing in the center, with other members of Pi Kappa Phi, 1919.

Wolfe, standing in the center, with other members of the Golden Fleece, in 1919. He was elected to membership in this oldest and foremost honor society at Chapel Hill in the spring of that year.

Wolfe at Chapel Hill, 1919.

Wolfe in front of Swain Hall during his final year at Chapel Hill, 1920.

Wolfe's diploma, dated June 16, 1920.

The President, Professors, and Board of Trustees
of the
University of North Carolina

TO ALL TO WHOM THESE PRESENTS SHALL COME

Greeting:

Whereas it is the ancient right and duty of Universities to reward meritorious attainments in Scholarship, and whereas

Thomas Clayton Wolfe

has honorably fulfilled the requirements imposed by the University now, therefore, We, under the authority of the Constitution of the State of North Carolina, have with due form admitted him to the degree of **Bachelor of Arts** granting therewith all the rights, honors, and privileges thereunto appertaining.

In witness whereof the Seal of the University and the signatures of the President, Professors, and Board of Trustees are hereunto affixed. Given at Chapel Hill in the State of North Carolina, this 16th day of June in the year of Our Lord 1920 and of this University the 125th

H. W. Chase, President
Trustees:

Professors:
Thos. J. Wilson Jr., Registrar.

North Carolina Library

8. Harvard University, 1920–1923

After graduating from the University of North Carolina in 1920, Wolfe attended Harvard University for three years in order to study playwriting in Professor George Pierce Baker's 47 Workshop. He earned his master's degree in 1922 but remained on for a year to continue his studies. The 47 Workshop presented two of Wolfe's plays at the Agassiz Theater at Radcliffe College. While at Harvard, Wolfe became friendly with Kenneth Raisbeck, Professor Baker's assistant. During those three years, Wolfe lived at five different addresses in Cambridge, Massachusetts.

George Pierce Baker, professor of drama at Harvard, in a photograph taken on February 23, 1920. In **Of Time and the River**, Wolfe calls him James Graves Hatcher, a man whose "appearance was imposing . . . [a] cultured man of the world."

Pack Library

Wolfe at Harvard, 1921.

North Carolina Library

North Carolina Library

Wolfe and Kenneth Raisbeck, Baker's assistant, in 1921. In **Of Time and the River***, Eugene Gant, Wolfe's fictional counterpart, is shocked to discover that Francis Starwick, the counterpart to Raisbeck, is a homosexual.*

When Wolfe earned his master's degree, the **Asheville Citizen** *announced to its readers, "Asheville Boy Wins Degree at Harvard: Thomas Wolfe Is Graduated from Widely Known University at Commencement Exercises."*

North Carolina Library

Maute

Maute

Wolfe's first residence in Cambridge was at 48 Buckingham Street, where he shared the top floor with three other recent graduates of the University of North Carolina. Albert Coates, T. Skinner Kittrell, and William T. Polk were all students at the Harvard Law School.

Wolfe remained in Cambridge during the summer of 1921 after completing his first year at Harvard. He studied English history at summer school and paid four dollars a week for his room at 42 Kirkland Street.

Maute

Wolfe's third residence in Cambridge was at 67 Hammond Street, where he spent a good deal of time alone during the 1921–1922 academic year.

Maute

During the 1922–1923 academic year, Wolfe lived at 21 Trowbridge Street.

Maute

Wolfe stayed at 10 Trowbridge Street for a short time during the winter of 1923–1924 before leaving for New York, where he began teaching at New York University on February 1, 1924.

9. First Years in New York, First Trip to Europe, 1923–1924

In August 1923 Wolfe submitted *Welcome to Our City* to the Theatre Guild, hoping for a Broadway production. The play was rejected, and Wolfe accepted a position in the English department of New York University. He began to teach in February 1924 while living at the Hotel Albert. Often, he spent weekends in Rhinebeck, New York, at the family home of Olin Dows, whom he had met at Harvard and whom he portrayed in *Of Time and the River* as Joel Pierce. At the end of the 1924 summer term, Wolfe traveled to Europe. On his voyage home, he met Aline Bernstein.

New-York Historical Society

*Wolfe lived in Room 2220 of the Hotel Albert during his first year in New York. In **Of Time and the River**, he calls it the Hotel Leopold.*

Teicher

Wolfe taught in this building, the Washington Square College of New York University.

Sign for the Hotel Albert.

Pack Library

Olin Dows's family mansion in Rhinebeck, New York, where Wolfe spent many weekends during 1924, was named Fox Hollow. The two-thousand-acre property overlooks the Hudson River, near the Roosevelt and Astor estates. In **Of Time and the River**, Wolfe referred to it as Far Field Farm. It is now a drug rehabilitation center.

Cleary

During one of Wolfe's visits to Fox Hollow, this photograph was taken. Left to right: Alice Dows, mother; Olin Dows; Elsie Benkard, first cousin; Margaret Dows, sister (Rosalind in **Of Time and the River**); and Wolfe. Members of the Thomas Wolfe Society found the picture in a Dows family album. This copy was made on June 6, 1986.

Cleary

Mariners' Museum

For the first of his seven trips to Europe, Wolfe left New York aboard the **Lancastria** on October 25, 1924. He landed in Southampton on November 5, and his passage cost $130.

In August 1925, Wolfe returned to New York on the **Olympic**. In **The Web and the Rock**, he calls this ship the **Vesuvia**: "A great panther of the sea, a proud swift cat of Italy. . . . She was a mighty ship." At the end of the voyage, he met Aline Bernstein.

Mariners' Museum

Aline Bernstein at work as a stage designer in 1938.

Aline Bernstein in 1953.

Tom and Aline—Look Homeward II, painted in 1988 by Jean-Pierre Pique. The original is in the Aldo P. Magi Collection.

Magi

10. Writing *Look Homeward, Angel*, New York and Europe, 1925–1928

During the 1925–1926 academic year, while Wolfe taught at New York University, his affair with Aline Bernstein flourished. When the term ended in June 1926, they traveled to Europe together. After visiting Paris and Chartres, they went to the Lake District of England, where Wolfe began to write *Look Homeward, Angel*. Aline Bernstein returned home in August 1926, and Wolfe moved into a London flat, where he continued to write. During the ensuing months, Wolfe traveled to the Continent twice and spent a few weeks in Oxford before sailing for home on December 22, 1926. He taught at New York University during the spring semester of 1927 while working on his novel. On July 12, he left for Europe again, spending two months there, some of the time with Aline Bernstein. He came home in time to teach throughout the 1927–1928 academic year. As soon as classes were finished, he went to Europe for the fourth time, remaining for the last half of 1928. One of the places he visited was Munich, where he was injured in a brawl at the Oktoberfest, an incident he described in *The Web and the Rock*.

 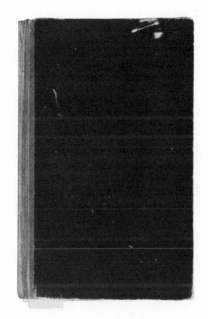 

Schneider and Houghton Library

Ledgers purchased for Wolfe by Aline Bernstein in which he began to write the book that became **Look Homeward, Angel**.

During August and September 1926, Wolfe lived at 32 Wellington Square in London. This photograph and the following two were taken in 1984

Teicher

Teicher

The interior of 32 Wellington Square, which Wolfe described in a letter dated September 3, 1926, to Henry Fisk Carlton, a fellow instructor at New York University, as "two rooms, a bedroom and an ample sitting room . . . in a house that looks exactly like all the other houses in Wellington Square" (**The Letters of Thomas Wolfe**, ed. Elizabeth Nowell).

The view toward the garden from Wolfe's flat at 32 Wellington Square.

Teicher

Wolfe stayed at Hilltop Farm in Oxford in October 1926 and wrote about it in "The House of the Far and Lost," originally published as a short story and later incorporated into **Of Time and the River**.

Pether

Cleary

Cleary

During the 1927–1928 academic year, Wolfe lived at 263 West Eleventh Street in New York. Aline Bernstein paid half the monthly rent of $135 and used the front room for her work.

The Harvard Club in New York, where Wolfe often stopped to read and write letters and collect his mail.

Wilson

Wilson

Wolfe enjoyed visiting European museums. One of his favorites was the Alte Pinakothek in Munich, where he particularly liked the paintings by Brueghel.

The entrance to the Oktoberfest as it appeared in 1988. Wolfe was there in 1928.

Wilson

Wilson

"The great red facade of the Löwenbrau Brewery, with its proud crest of two royal lions rampant . . . [is one of] the great beer halls erected by the famous breweries. . . . Thousands of people were roaring over their beer at the tables, and hundreds more milled up and down incessantly, looking for an opening" (**The Web and the Rock**).

An Oktoberfest beer hall with a "thousand beery faces . . . in that vast and murky hall . . . the image of savage faces in the old dark forest of barbaric time" (**The Web and the Rock**).

*A ride at the Oktoberfest, part of "the elaborate machinery for making one dizzy" (**The Web and the Rock**).*

Wilson

11. Publication of *Look Homeward, Angel,* 1928–1929

In March 1928, Wolfe completed his novel and turned it over to Aline Bernstein to find a publisher. A month later, it was rejected by Boni and Liveright. The manuscript was then given to a literary agent, Madeline Boyd, who placed it with Charles Scribner's Sons. In January 1929, shortly after Wolfe returned to New York from his fourth trip to Europe, he met Maxwell Perkins of Scribner's, who accepted the manuscript for publication. The close relationship established between Perkins and Wolfe during the editing of *Look Homeward, Angel* continued until Wolfe's death, although it was partially severed when Wolfe left Scribner's for Harper and Brothers nine months before he died. Wolfe's first novel was published October 18, 1929.

Pack Library

Maxwell Perkins, Wolfe's editor,
mentor, and friend.

Perkins and Fred Wolfe, New York, 1943.

Braden-Hatchett

Cleary

Cleary

The Perkins home on Elm Street in New Canaan, Connect-icut, where Wolfe was a frequent visitor. Perkins joked that there was a pillar for each of his daughters to lean against while waiting for suitors.

A present-day train at the New Canaan station where Wolfe would get off and walk up the hill to the Perkins house.

*Wolfe on a visit to Asheville in the summer of 1929, shortly before the publication of **Look Homeward, Angel**. Because of the negative reception the book received in his hometown, this was to be Wolfe's last visit to Asheville for eight years.*

North Carolina Library

*Just before and just following the publication of **Look Homeward, Angel**, Wolfe lived at 27 West Fifteenth Street in New York.*

Pack Librar

{ CONTINUED FROM FRONT FLAP }

an inevitable fruition in beauty. And the book has in it sin and terror and darkness—ugly dry lusts, cruelty—the dark, the evil, the forbidden. But I believe it has many other things as well, and I wrote it with strong joy, without counting the costs, for I was sure at the time that the whole of my intention which was to come simply and unsparingly to naked life, and to tell all of my story without affectation would be apparent.

"When I wrote the book I seized with delight everything that would give it color and richness. All the variety and madness of the characters—the cruel waste, the dark flowering evil of life I wrote about with as much exultancy as the health, sanity, joy.

"The book is fiction—it is loaded with invention: story, fantasy, vision. But it is a fiction that is, I believe, more true than fact—a fiction that grew out of a life completely digested in my spirit, a fiction which telescopes, condenses, and objectifies all the random or incompleted gestures of life—which tries to comprehend people, in short, not by telling what people did, but what they should have done.

"What merit it has I do not know. It sometimes seems to me that it presents a picture of American life that I have never seen elsewhere."

THOMAS WOLFE

From a photograph by Doris Ulmann.

THOMAS WOLFE, author of "Look Homeward, Angel" was born in Asheville, North Carolina, in 1900. In 1920 he was graduated from the University of North Carolina and three years later received his Master of Arts degree from Harvard University, where he worked with George Pierce Baker in the 47 Workshop, following up dramatic experience as a member of the Playmakers at North Carolina. "Look Homeward, Angel" was begun while the author was staying in England and the news that his manuscript would be published reached Mr. Wolfe three years later in Vienna. At present he is teaching in New York University.

Conspicuous books of our day have, like "Look Homeward, Angel", revealed the life of the small American city. But they have shown it as dull, arid, drab. Mr. Wolfe's book shows that whatever the state of ethics and culture—this life burns with the deep colors of human emotions and richly marked characters.

LOOK
HOMEWARD,
ANGEL
▼
WOLFE

LOOK HOMEWARD,
ANGEL
—
THOMAS WOLFE

SCRIBNERS

$2.50

LOOK HOMEWARD, ANGEL

By
THOMAS WOLFE

The character and quality of this unusual novel may best be shown by an excerpt from a letter by the author which accompanied the manuscript when it was submitted to the publishers:

"The book covers the life of a large family (the Gants of Altamount) for a period of twenty years. It tries to describe not only the visible outer lives of all these people, but even more their buried lives.

"This book was written in simpleness and nakedness of soul. When I began to write the book twenty months ago I got back something of a child's innocency and wonder. It has in it much that to me is painful and ugly, but, without sentimentality or dishonesty, it seems to me that pain has

{ CONTINUED ON BACK FLAP OF THIS JACKET }

*The dust jacket for the first edition of **Look Homeward, Angel**.*

*The Asheville press gave a good deal of attention to the publication of **Look Homeward, Angel**.*

North Carolina Library

Thomas Wolfe as photographed by Doris Ulmann, about 1929.

12. Further Travels, Writing *Of Time and the River*, 1930–1935

Having been awarded a Guggenheim Fellowship, Wolfe spent almost a year in Europe, from May 1930 to March 1931. On his return, he rented the first of four apartments in Brooklyn. During the next four years, he worked on *Of Time and the River*, taking breaks for short trips to Tannersville, New York; Maine; Montreal; York Springs, Pennsylvania; Bermuda; Washington, D.C.; and Chicago. Six days before *Of Time and the River* was published, Wolfe left for Europe, wanting to be away when the book appeared.

Pack Library

Wolfe's residence in London during the fall of 1930 was at 75 Ebury Street.

Wolfe lived in a basement apartment at 40 Verandah Place in Brooklyn from March to October 1931. Aline Bernstein visited him here every Thursday.

Cleary

Wolfe with Mrs. L. Effingham de Forest at her summer home at Onteora Park, in the Catskills, Tannersville, New York, September 1931. Wolfe met the de Forests through Alfred Dashiell, editor of **Scribner's Magazine***, and they became friends.*

Pack Library

Wolfe at Onteora Park in September 1931.

*Wolfe with L. Effingham de Forest at Onteora Park,
September 1931.*

Cleary

Wolfe lived in a third-floor apartment at 111 Columbia Heights in Brooklyn from November 1931 until August 1932. Here, Wolfe's mother came to visit him and had a confrontation with Aline Bernstein, following which he made a definitive break in the love affair.

Wolfe lived at 101 Columbia Heights in Brooklyn from August 1932 until October 1933, working on the book that was to become **Of Time and the River**.

Pack Library

Pack Library

Wolfe lived in a second-floor apartment at 5 Montague Terrace in Brooklyn from October 1933 to March 1935. He continued to write until Christmas 1934, when he finally turned his manuscript over to Perkins. At its fourth annual meeting in 1983, the Thomas Wolfe Society placed a bronze plaque at the entrance to this building to commemorate Wolfe's residence here while he wrote **Of Time and the River**.

Wolfe at 5 Montague Terrace after completing **Of Time and the River**.

Pack Library

Elizabeth Nowell became Wolfe's literary agent in January 1934. Later, she was his first biographer and the editor of his letters. This photograph was taken in 1960 by Norman Fortier for use in publicizing her biography of Wolfe.

Pack Library

North Carolina Library

Wolfe in 1934 with part of the seven-hundred-thousand-word manuscript for **Of Time and the River**.

Wolfe's travel record from his notebooks showing that he started to travel at the age of four and that he covered nearly 150,000 miles in the next thirty years, visiting two-thirds of the states and much of Europe.

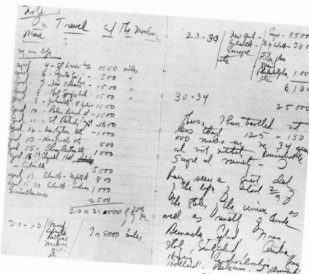

Houghton Library

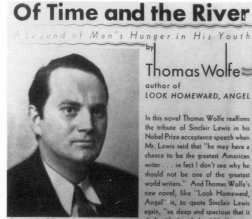

The dust jacket for **Of Time and the River**, *published March 8, 1935.*

*Wolfe in the offices of Charles Scribner's Sons for the publication of **Of Time and the River**.*

North Carolina Library, photograph by Jerome Zerbe

North Carolina Library

Wolfe in Berlin, May 1935.

North Carolina Library

Wolfe in Germany, May 1935. During his sixth trip to Europe, from March 2 to July 4, 1935, he visited England, Germany, and Denmark.

Wolfe in Copenhagen, June 21, 1935.

*Wolfe with Dr. Russel V. Lee aboard the **Bremen**. During his voyage to New York from June 27 to July 4, 1935, Wolfe became friendly with Dr. Lee, whom he later visited at his home in Palo Alto, California.*

Houghton Library

North Carolina Library

Pack Library

*Wolfe with the **Bremen**'s captain. The other men are not identified.*

Pack Library

*Aboard the **Bremen**, July 3, 1935. Left to right: unidentified, Dr. Russel V. Lee, the ship's captain, unidentified, Wolfe. On the table is a copy of the newly published **Of Time and the River**.*

Two portraits of Thomas Wolfe by Georges Schreiber, about 1935.

Thomas Wolfe

Houghton Library

Thomas Wolfe

Houghton Library

13. First Trip West and Last Trip to Europe, 1935–1936

In the summer of 1935, Wolfe participated in the Colorado Writers' Conference in Boulder and then traveled through New Mexico, Utah, and California. On the way home, he stopped in St. Louis to find the house where his brother Grover had died in 1904. Back in New York, he rented an apartment at 865 First Avenue; two months later, in November 1935, a collection of his short stories, *From Death to Morning,* was published. Wolfe continued to write, and in April 1936 *The Story of a Novel,* based on his lecture at the Colorado Writers' Conference, was published. On July 23, 1936, Wolfe sailed for his seventh and last trip to Europe. He attended the Olympic Games in Berlin and became more and more disenchanted with the Germans. He arrived back in New York on September 24, 1936.

Houghton Library

Wolfe at the Colorado Writers' Conference, August 1935.

Wolfe with Theodore Davison, the organizer of the conference.

Pack Library

Wolfe in Central City, Colorado, August 10, 1935.

Wolfe and Helen R. Ferril, the wife of Thomas Hornsby Ferril, a Western poet admired by Wolfe. Wolfe visited the Ferrils in Denver in August 1935, and they then drove him through Rocky Mountain National Park.

Wolfe and Desmond Powell, August 1935. After visiting the Ferrils, Wolfe traveled to Colorado Springs to see Powell, a former colleague from New York University.

Wolfe in Salt Lake City, where he stopped in September 1935 on his way back to New York.

North Carolina Library

Another view of Wolfe in Salt Lake City, September 1935.

Wolfe kept an apartment at 865 First Avenue in New York for two years from the fall of 1935 to the fall of 1937. It was two blocks from Perkins's New York home, which Wolfe visited often, even though his relationship with Perkins was becoming increasingly strained.

Cleary

North Carolina Library

The dust jacket for **From Death to Morning**, *published November 14, 1935.*

Thomas Wolfe, 1935, a pencil drawing by Edward A. Raffel, Cleveland, Ohio, 1990.

Magi

Wolfe in 1936.

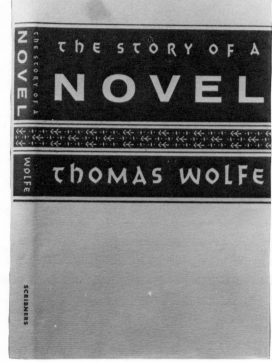

North Carolina Library

Houghton Library

*The dust jacket for **The Story of a Novel**, published April 21, 1936.*

Cultural Resources and Marie Gorsline

Thomas Wolfe in 1936, by Douglas Gorsline. The original hangs in the Thomas Wolfe Memorial in Asheville. Wolfe sat five times for this portrait. Gorsline's drawings and paintings were later used in an illustrated edition of **Look Homeward, Angel***. His first wife was one of Maxwell Perkins's daughters.*

Pack Library

Wolfe in the Austrian Tirol during his final trip to Europe in the summer of 1936.

14. You Can Go Home Again: Return to Asheville, 1937

In April 1937, exhausted by the strain of arguments with Perkins and brooding about his health, Wolfe decided that the time had finally come to pay his first visit to Asheville since the publication of *Look Homeward, Angel*. He was apprehensive about his reception but relieved to be warmly welcomed after he arrived on May 3, 1937. He rented a cabin at Oteen, on the outskirts of Asheville, and spent the summer of 1937 there.

Wolfe and his mother on the steps of the Old Kentucky Home, May 1937.

North Carolina Library; photograph by Elliot Lyman Fisher

Wolfe during his visit to Asheville in the summer of 1937, at the doorway of 161 Kimberly Avenue, the home of Mabel and Ralph Wheaton.

Braden-Hatchett

Wolfe and his brother Fred in July 1937 at the home of their sister Effie Gambrell in Anderson, South Carolina.

North Carolina Library

Braden-Hatchett

The Wolfes in the yard of the Old Kentucky Home in the summer of 1937. Left to right: Effie Wolfe Gambrell, Frank Wolfe, Julia Wolfe, Thomas Wolfe, Mabel Wolfe Wheaton, Fred Wolfe, and first cousin Ollie Wolfe.

Pack Library

Another photograph taken in the yard of the Old Kentucky Home in the summer of 1937. Left to right: Thomas Wolfe, Julia Wolfe, Frank Wolfe, Effie Wolfe Gambrell, Fred Wolfe, Mabel Wolfe Wheaton, and Ralph Wheaton.

Braden-Hatchett

The Wolfes on the porch at the Kimberly Avenue home of Mabel and Ralph Wheaton in the summer of 1937. Left to right: Thomas Wolfe, Effie Wolfe Gambrell, Julia Wolfe, Mabel Wolfe Wheaton, Frank Wolfe, and Fred Wolfe.

Pack Library

The cabin at Oteen that Wolfe rented for the summer of 1937 at a rate of thirty dollars a month. The cabin belonged to Max Whitson, a former classmate of Wolfe's at the North State Fitting School and at the University of North Carolina.

The Oteen cabin today.

Teicher

Wolfe at the Oteen cabin in the summer of 1937.

Wolfe working in the Oteen cabin.

Pack Library

Pack Library

Pack Library

The steady stream of visitors to the Oteen cabin made it difficult for Wolfe to work but signaled his acceptance by the people of Asheville, so he always welcomed them.

Thomas Wolfe as painted by Betty Ann Mills in 1946. In 1937, then a thirteen-year-old aspiring artist, Mills sat near Wolfe in an Asheville restaurant and drew a sketch that Wolfe autographed for her. In 1946, based on the sketch, her memory, and a photo of Wolfe, she painted this portrait, which now hangs in the Thomas Wolfe Room of the University of North Carolina at Chapel Hill.

Pack Library

Wolfe in front of the courthouse in Burnsville, North Carolina, during the summer of 1937. He was called to testify about a shooting fracas he had accidentally witnessed during a stop in Burnsville on his way to Asheville. This claim on his time, added to those made by his visitors, irritated him, and he left Asheville on a sour note in September 1937, not to return until his funeral.

15. Last months in New York, September 1937– May 1938

After returning to New York in September 1937, Wolfe rented an apartment on the eighth floor of the Hotel Chelsea. He ended his association with Scribner's and, on December 31, 1937, signed a contract with Harper and Brothers. Wolfe had already become friendly with Edward Aswell, who was to be his editor at Harper and Brothers, and he had spent Christmas 1937 at the Aswell home in Chappaqua, New York.

The entrance to the Hotel Chelsea, Wolfe's final home in New York.

Door to Suite 829, Wolfe's apartment in the Hotel Chelsea. It consisted of a bedroom, a living room, a bathroom, and a small room in which his secretary worked.

Charcoal drawing of Thomas Wolfe at the Hotel Chelsea in 1938, by Soss Melik.

National Portrait Gallery

Edward Aswell, who edited Wolfe's three posthumous books.

Pack Library

Cleary

Doll

The Aswell house in Chappaqua, New York, where Wolfe spent Christmas 1937 and where he visited on a few other occasions.

Another view of the Aswell house.

16. Last Trip to the West, May–September 1938

On May 17, 1938, Wolfe delivered to Aswell two bundles of manuscript and left New York for Lafayette, Indiana, where he lectured at Purdue University. He then spent a weekend in Chicago before going on to Denver, where he remained for a week, visiting friends from his earlier visit. His next stop was Portland, Oregon, where he stayed at the University Club. During the two weeks he was in Portland he made a short visit to Seattle that included a ferry ride to Port Townsend. In Portland, Wolfe met Edward M. Miller of the *Portland Oregonian* and Ray Conway of the Oregon Automobile Association, who were planning a two-week tour of the national parks to show how visitors could enjoy the parks without spending much time or money. Wolfe accepted Miller's invitation to join them. The trip lasted from June 20 to July 2, 1938.

Pack Library

Wolfe in Denver, May 1938.

Braden-Hatchett

Wolfe crossing Puget Sound on the ferry to Port Towns-end, June 17, 1938.

Wolfe on a log pond at the Pope and Talbot Mill, Port Gamble, Washington, June 1938.

Another view of Wolfe at the Pope and Talbot Mill.

North Carolina Library

Wolfe with a fish he caught along the Washougal River near Camas, Washington, just north of Portland. While in Portland, Wolfe met Warren Wright, manager of the book department of the J. K. Gill Company, and accepted Wright's invitation to spend a few days at his cabin.

The start of the national parks tour, June 20, 1938. Standing in front of the University Club in Portland and near the white Ford used for the trip are, from left to right, Ray Conway, Thomas Wolfe, and Edward M. Miller.

Pack Library

Wolfe feeding a chipmunk during the national parks tour.

Wolfe at Yosemite National Park, June 22, 1938.

North Carolina Library

Wolfe at the Grand Canyon, June 24, 1938.

North Carolina Library

Wolfe at Yellowstone National Park, June 28, 1938.

17. Death

When the national parks tour ended on July 2, 1938, Wolfe went to Seattle, where Theresa and James F. Stevens introduced him to a number of their friends. Wolfe had met the Stevenses through Stuart Holbrook, a leading northwestern author who had looked after Wolfe when he first arrived in Portland on June 7. Stevens was a public relations officer for the West Coast Lumberman's Association and was admired by Wolfe for his rendition of the Paul Bunyan stories. He and his wife held several parties for Wolfe, and, when Wolfe became ill, they arranged for him to see their family doctor, Edward C. Ruge. Ruge's diagnosis was pneumonia, and he admitted Wolfe to his private sanatorium, Firlawns. A month later, when Wolfe had not responded to treatment, he was transferred to Providence Hospital in Seattle, where his physicians included Dr. John Dawson and Dr. Charles E. Watts. Their diagnosis was tuberculosis. Wolfe became delirious and increasingly ill. Because the tuberculosis had invaded his brain, Dr. George W. Swift, a brain surgeon, was called in for consultation. He recommended that Wolfe be seen by Dr. Walter Dandy at Johns Hopkins Hospital in Baltimore. Dandy operated and found incurable miliary tuberculosis of the brain. Wolfe died on September 15, 1938. His body was taken to Asheville, where the funeral was held in the First Presbyterian Church. Wolfe was buried in the family plot at Riverside Cemetery.

North Carolina Library

Wolfe at the home of Theresa and James F. Stevens on July 4, 1938. Left to right: Margaret Haglund, James F. Stevens, Thomas Wolfe, Ivar Haglund, and Theresa Stevens.

Detail of the previous photograph, showing a close-up of Wolfe in the last clear picture taken of him.

Braden-Hatchett

Dr. Edward C. Ruge, who mistakenly treated Wolfe for pneumonia at his private sanatorium, Firlawns. In view of the final diagnosis of Wolfe's condition, it is ironic that Ruge had been a tuberculosis specialist, even though, at the time he saw Wolfe, his specialization was nervous and mental diseases.

Port

Port

Firlawns Sanatorium in Kenmore, Washington, twelve miles north of Seattle, where Wolfe stayed for a month until August 6, 1938, when he was admitted to Providence Hospital.

Stevens Papers

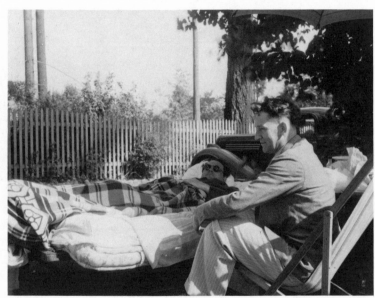

Stevens Papers

Wolfe (lying down at right) at Firlawns Sanatorium on July 23, 1938.

Another view of Wolfe at Firlawns on July 23.

Sisters of Providence

Providence Hospital, where Wolfe was a patient from
August 6 to September 5, 1938.

Dr. John Dawson, one of the doctors who treated
Wolfe at Providence Hospital.

Sisters of Providence

The medical staff at Providence Hospital in 1925. Dr. Dawson is seated on the right, second from the front. Dr. Swift is seated on the left, second from the back.

Sisters of Providence

PAGE								YEAR	
632								1938	

Admitted	Room	at	Name	Maiden Name	Residence		Phone		
Aug. 6	202	42.00	Mr. Thomas Wolfe		Harper & Bros. Publishers, New York City				

Discharged	Age	Date of Birth	Birth Place	Religion	Social Status	Complaint	Employment
9/5	37	Oct. 3	N. Carolina	Prot.	S.	Med.	Harper

Father	Birth Place	Mother	Address	Birth Place	Phone	Previous History	Terms
William	Penn.	Judy E. Westall		N. Carolina			

Relative or Friend

Brother- Fred W.- New Hungerford Hotel, El 3900

Case No.	Physician
3730	Dr. E.C. Roggi & Watts

30 Days .... Days ....

Surgery .... Medicine .... 11 45 .... Laboratory 6 00

Dressings.......... X-Ray 8/8 10 10 8/17- 10.00 8/26-10.—

Physio 62 00   9/5 - 25 00

Responsible   Self.

DEBIT		CREDIT		CREDIT
	180.00	8/17/38	R 60.10	
			L 5.00	
	17.45		XR 10.00	
	55.00	8/27/38	R 66.00	
			L 1.00	
			X 20.00	
	62.00	9/5/38	Phy 47.50	
			104.95	
PAID 314 45			314 45	

Sisters of Providence

Wolfe's final bill from Providence Hospital, dated September 5, 1938.

Johns Hopkins Hospital as it appeared in 1938, when Wolfe died there.

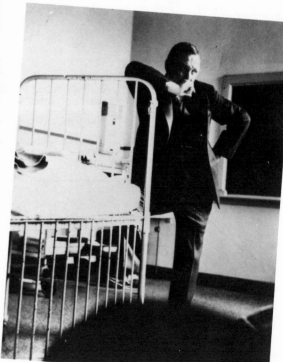

At the time of Wolfe's death, Dr. Walter Dandy was reputed to be the foremost brain surgeon in the United States. After Wolfe died, the family protested Dandy's $1,500 bill. Perkins, as executor of Wolfe's estate, persuaded him to accept $500.

Johns Hopkins Hospital

When his brother died, Fred Wolfe is said to have cursed the Christ statue that stands in the entrance rotunda of the Johns Hopkins Hospital.

Wolfe's casket being taken from the First Presbyterian Church in Asheville following his funeral service.

Pack Library

The active pallbearers in Wolfe's funeral procession were Paul Green, Albert Coates, Frederick Koch, Jonathan Daniels, Hamilton Basso, Henry Westall, J. Y. Jordan, Jr., and W. O. Wolfe, Jr. Behind the coffin are Julia Wolfe, Fred Wolfe, Mr. and Mrs. Fred Gambrell, and other members of the family.

Pack Library

Stites

Teicher

Wolfe's casket at Riverside Cemetery.

The Wolfe family plot at Riverside Cemetery.

Teicher

Teicher

Teicher

The tombstones for W. O. Wolfe and Julia Wolfe, Mabel Wolfe Wheaton and Ralph Wheaton, and Thomas Wolfe. The epigraphs on Thomas's tombstone are "The last voyage, the longest, the best," from **Look Homeward, Angel**, and "Death bent to touch his chosen son with mercy, love and pity, and put the seal of honor on him when he died," from **The Web and the Rock**.

Teicher

This plaque was placed at the entrance to Riverside Cemetery on May 14, 1988, by the Thomas Wolfe Society to commemorate the fiftieth anniversary of Wolfe's death.

CREDO

Something has spoken to me in the night, burning the tapers of the waning year; something has spoken in the night, and told me I shall die, I know not where. Saying:

"To lose the earth you know, for greater knowing; to lose the life you have, for greater life; to leave the friends you loved, for greater loving; to find a land more kind than home, more large than earth—

"—Whereon the pillars of this earth are founded, toward which the conscience of the world is tending—a wind is rising, and the rivers flow."

—*You Can't Go Home Again*

Magi

*The credo from **You Can't Go Home Again**.*

18. Posthumous Publications

After Wolfe died, his editor at Harper and Brothers fashioned three books out of the manuscript that Wolfe had left before setting out on his final trip: *The Web and the Rock, You Can't Go Home Again,* and *The Hills Beyond.*

The dust jacket for **The Web and the Rock**, published June 22, 1939.

The dust jacket for **You Can't Go Home Again**, published September 18, 1940

Thomas Wolfe

Thomas Wolfe was born on October 3rd, 1900, in Asheville, N. C. Educated at the University of North Carolina and at Harvard, he wanted to be a writer, and his first efforts were directed toward the theatre. He wrote several plays, but, failing to find a producer for them, he turned his interest toward other literary forms.

Look Homeward, Angel, his first novel, brought him instant recognition when it was published in 1929. And six years later *Of Time and the River* established him securely as one of the most powerful and authentic voices of his generation. Within the following year he published two other books, a collection of stories, *From Death to Morning*, and an illuminating account of his creative methods, *The Story of a Novel*.

By 1936 Wolfe had completed what he looked upon as his period of apprenticeship, and was ready to embark upon a vast new enterprise—a novel or a series of novels (he did not yet know which) into which he wanted to pack everything he had learned about life. Through several years he labored strenuously at it, working from twelve to fourteen hours a day, and as the manuscript took shape it grew into two novels, both of which were finished and turned over to his publishers in May, 1938. His work done, his mind at peace, he then left New York for a vacation in the Pacific Northwest. There, early in July, he became ill with pneumonia, from the complications of which he died at Johns Hopkins Hospital in Baltimore on September 15th, 1938.

The first of his posthumous novels was *The Web and the Rock*, published in 1939. The second is *You Can't Go Home Again*, which represents Wolfe's latest and maturest work.

THE CRITICS PROCLAIM HIM ONE OF AMERICA'S IMMORTALS

"Wolfe wrote as one inspired. No one in his generation had his command of language, his passion, his energy."—Clifton Fadiman in *The New Yorker*.

"Wolfe wrote not only with passion and conviction, but also with the truest sort of vision, of the life he had known and seen. He was, in my opinion, one of the greatest novelists of all time. And, in this posthumous book, my regard for his genius increases."—Burton Rascoe in *Newsweek*.

(Continued on back flap)

No. 1897

You Can't Go Home Again

A Novel about a Lost Modern Who Found Himself

BY

THOMAS WOLFE

AUTHOR OF "LOOK HOMEWARD, ANGEL," "OF TIME AND THE RIVER," AND "THE WEB AND THE ROCK"

THOMAS WOLFE

You Can't Go Home Again

HARPER   HARPER & BROTHERS · ESTABLISHED 1817

North Carolina Library

*The dust jacket for **The Hills Beyond**, published October 15, 1941.*

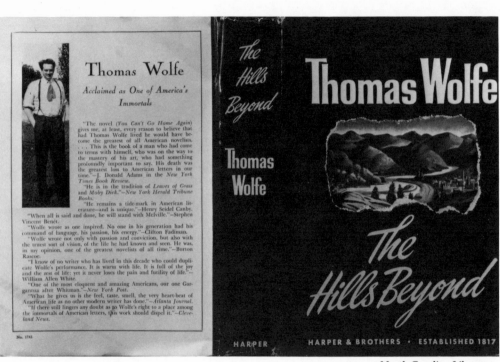

19. A Portfolio of Portraits

The drawing of Thomas Wolfe used by Scribner's
to advertise his books, date unknown.

Magi

Magi

Pencil drawing by Charles T. Mayer, Sandusky, Ohio. 1971.

Magi

Pencil drawing by Charles T. Mayer, 1975.

Oil painting by Daniel P. Fisher, Candler, North Carolina, 1976. The original hangs in the Thomas Wolfe Auditorium, Asheville, North Carolina.

Teicher

North Carolina Library; photograph by Jerry Cotten

*Frank Mason of New York photographed
with his oil painting of Wolfe, 1979.*

North Carolina Library

Print by Michele Chessare, 1979.

Magi

Drawing by Carl J. Samson, 1981.

Drawing by Jeannene Jesionek Chestner, 1981.

THOMAS WOLFE
1900 - 1938

Magi

Drawing by Jeannene Jesionek Chestner, date unknown.

Magi

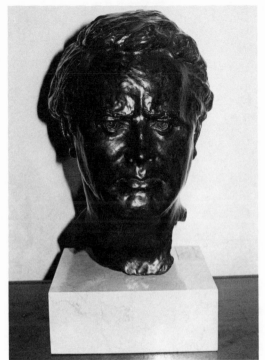

Bronze cast by William E. Hipp III, date unknown, owned by the John Motley Morehead Foundation, Chapel Hill, North Carolina.

North Carolina Library

Bronze cast by Nat Werner, date unknown, owned by the North Carolina Collection, University of North Carolina Library, Chapel Hill.

North Carolina Library

North Carolina Library

Plaster cast by Nat Werner used for making the bronze head in the North Carolina Collection.

Stites

Thomas Wolfe as Loo... Homeward, Angel, by *John Sokol, 1990.*

Photographs, dates unknown.

Sites

Source unknown

Although obviously not a portrait of
Wolfe, this picture of the Liberty ship
Thomas Wolfe, launched in 1943, is
a fitting conclusion to the story of
Wolfe's life. He was an inveterate
traveler, crossing the Atlantic fourteen times and visiting all corners
of the United States. It was most
appropriate to name a ship for him,
symbolizing the words on his tombstone: "The last voyage, the longest,
the best."

Peabody Museum

Chronology

1900   Thomas Wolfe born October 3 at 92 Woodfin Street, Asheville, North Carolina, to Julia Elizabeth Westall Wolfe and William Oliver Wolfe. Youngest of eight children.

1904   Grover Cleveland Wolfe, twin brother of Benjamin Harrison Wolfe, dies November 16 in St. Louis, where Julia runs a boardinghouse, the North Carolina, at 5095 Fairmount Avenue, during the World's Fair.

1906   On August 30, mother buys the Old Kentucky Home at 48 Spruce Street, Asheville. In September enters Orange Street Public School, Asheville.

1909   Visits New Orleans and Hot Springs, Arkansas, with mother.

1912   In September enters North State Fitting School, established by Mr. and Mrs. J. M. Roberts. Mrs. Roberts (Margaret) will be a major influence.

1913   Attends March 4 inauguration of Woodrow Wilson in Washington, D.C.

1916   Completes college preparatory course on June 16, after winning gold medal for essay on Shakespeare. In September enters University of North Carolina at Chapel Hill. In December visits a brothel in Durham, North Carolina, for first sexual experience.

1917   During summer works in Asheville at National Cash Register office of brother-in-law Ralph Wheaton, husband of Mabel. Has romance with Clara Paul. Gains first publication in November with a poem entitled "A Field in Flanders" in *University of North Carolina Magazine*.

1918   Roommate Edmund Burdick dies in spring. Works for summer at a pier in Newport News, Virginia, loading grain and ammunition. In September enrolls in

Professor Frederick Koch's playwriting course at the University of North Carolina. Brother Ben dies October 19. In November becomes editor of *Tar Heel*, student newspaper at the University of North Carolina.

1919 Plays title role in his *Return of Buck Gavin*, staged March 14–15 by Carolina Playmakers. Wins Worth Prize in Philosophy in June for his essay "The Crisis in Industry." Spends summer in Asheville. In fall becomes editor-in-chief of *Tar Heel*. Play *The Third Night* presented by Carolina Playmakers December 12–13.

1920 Graduates June 16 from the University of North Carolina with Bachelor of Arts degree. Declines teaching job at the Bingham School, Asheville. In September enters Harvard University Graduate School of Arts and Sciences. Enrolls in Professor George Pierce Baker's 47 Workshop. Meets Kenneth Raisbeck, Baker's assistant. Lives at 48 Buckingham Street, Cambridge.

1921 Short version of play *The Mountains* presented by the 47 Workshop on January 25. In May completes three of four courses required for Master of Arts degree. Spends summer at 42 Kirkland Street, Cambridge. In September continues graduate studies at Harvard after brief visit to Baltimore, where father is being treated at Johns Hopkins Hospital. Lives at 67 Hammond Street. *The Mountains* presented as a full-length play October 21–22 by the 47 Workshop at Agassiz Theater, Radcliffe College.

1922 Receives Master of Arts degree from Harvard University in June. Father dies June 20. Spends summer in Asheville. Returns to Harvard and the 47 Workshop in September. Lives at 21 Trowbridge Street, Cambridge.

1923 *Welcome to Our City* presented May 11–23 by the 47 Workshop at the Agassiz Theater. During summer revises *Welcome to Our City* at Henry Carlton's summer home in New Hampshire. In August submits *Welcome to Our City* to Theatre Guild. In September goes to New York and lives with two University of North Carolina alumni at 439 West 123d Street. Works as a fundraiser for University of North Carolina. In December *Welcome to Our City* rejected by Theatre Guild.

1924 On January 10 applies to Professor Homer A. Watt, chairman, English Department, New York University, for a job teaching English. On February 1 begins to teach English at New York University. Lives at the Hotel Albert, Room 2220. Teaches summer term at New York University through September 5, spending weekends at Olin Dows's home, Fox Hollow, Rhinebeck, New York. Sails October 25 on *Lancastria* for the first of seven European trips. Lands November 5 in England. Visits Bath, Bristol, and London. In December manuscript of *Mannerhouse* stolen in a Paris pension on Rue de l'Université.

1925   Quarrels with Kenneth Raisbeck in January after spending a month in France with him, Marjorie Fairbanks, and Helen Harding. In February visits Chartres, Orleans, and Tours. In March accepts fall term appointment at New York University. From May to August visits Paris, northern Italy, England, and Switzerland. On July 19, *Asheville Citizen* publishes journal excerpt "London Tower." Returns to New York in August on the *Olympic*. Meets Aline Bernstein at the end of the voyage. In September resumes teaching at New York University. In October begins love affair with Aline Bernstein. Visits Asheville for Christmas.

1926   In January moves into loft at 13 East Eighth Street. During spring attempts to find producers for *Welcome to Our City* and *Mannerhouse*. Sails June 23 on the *Berengeria* for second trip to Europe. In July joins Aline Bernstein in Paris. Visits Chartres, London, and Bath. Begins to write *Look Homeward, Angel* (then called *O Lost*) at Ilkley and Ambleside, Lake District, England. During August lives at 32 Wellington Square, London. Continues writing *Look Homeward,*

Angel. Leaves London September 12 for two weeks in Belgium. Returns to England in October and rents rooms at Hilltop Farm, Oxford. In December makes first visit to Germany. Sails December 22 from Cherbourg on the *Majestic*. Arrives December 28 in New York. On New Year's Eve attends Fine Arts Ball with Aline Bernstein.

1927   Continues working on *Look Homeward, Angel* at 13 East Eighth Street. In March visits Boston. During spring works on *Look Homeward, Angel* at Olin Dows's home, Fox Hollow. Attends July Fourth fireworks display at Astor estate with the Dows family. Sails July 12 on the *George Washington* for third trip to Europe. Visits Paris, Strasbourg, Munich, Vienna, Prague, and Nuremberg with Aline Bernstein. Sails September 10 on the *Belgenland*. Arrives September 18 in New York. On September 20 resumes teaching at New York University. Lives at 263 West Eleventh Street.

1928   Finishes *Look Homeward, Angel* on March 31. Gives manuscript to Aline Bernstein to seek a publisher. Manuscript rejected April 30 by Boni and Liveright. Leaves manuscript with literary agent Madeline Boyd on May 22. Leaves New York June 10 for brief visit to Asheville following rift with Aline Bernstein. Sails June 30 on the *Rotterdam* for fourth trip to Europe. Lands July 9 in Boulogne to visit France, Belgium, Germany, Hungary, and Italy. Works on *The River People*. Injured September 30 in brawl at Munich Oktoberfest and hospitalized. Discharged from hospital October 4 after spending twenty-eighth birthday there. Arrives October 19 in Vienna after visiting Oberammergau, Germany. Receives letter October 22 from Madeline Boyd saying Scribner's is interested in *Look Homeward, Angel*. Leaves Vienna October 27 for two weeks in Budapest. Sails December 21 from Naples on the *Vulcania*. Lands New Year's Eve in New York.

1929   Reconciled with Aline Bernstein in January. Meets Maxwell Perkins. Scribner's accepts *Look Homeward, Angel*. Lives at 27 West Fifteenth Street, second floor. Beginning in February teaches half-time at New York University. Revises manuscript. In April changes title from *O Lost* to *Look Homeward, Angel*. In June visits Olin Dows at Fox Hollow. Reads proofs during summer in Boothbay Harbor, Maine. Visits Montreal and Quebec. "An Angel on the Porch" published by *Scribner's Magazine* in August. In September resumes teaching full-time at New York University after two-week visit to Asheville and Anderson, South Carolina. *Look Homeward, Angel* published October 18. Stock market crashes on "Black Thursday," October 24. Lectures to Women's Club, Glen Ridge, New Jersey, on November 1. On December 16 applies for Guggenheim Fellowship.

1930   Attends party January 3 at the Bernsteins with Alexander Calder performing (later satirized as "The Party at Jacks"). In February stops teaching at New York University. Awarded Guggenheim Fellowship March 30. In April visits Atlantic City, New Jersey, and Lancaster, Pennsylvania. Tension with Aline Bernstein increases. Sails May 10 on the *Volendam* for fifth trip to Europe. Arrives May 19 in Paris. Meets F. Scott Fitzgerald in Paris during June. Settles in Montreux on July 11 after visiting Avignon, Marseilles, Provence, and Geneva. British edition of *Look Homeward, Angel* published July 14. In September visits Germany and sees fighting between Nazis and Communists. Settles in London in October. Rents flat at 75 Ebury Street. Maintains steady regimen of writing. Mentioned favorably by Sinclair Lewis in his December 12 Nobel Prize acceptance speech, Stockholm.

1931   Meets Sinclair Lewis in London during February. Visits Holland. Sails home February 26 on the *Europa*. Lands March 4 in New York and settles in Brooklyn at 40 Verandah Place. Aline Bernstein attempts suicide April 1. Visits Maine during August. Kenneth Raisbeck found dead September 29 in a cemetery in

Westport, Connecticut, under mysterious circumstances. Moves November 1 to 111 Columbia Heights, Brooklyn.

1932   Breaks definitively with Aline Bernstein in January. In February completes *The Web of Earth*, a short novel. "A Portrait of Bascom Hawke" published in *Scribner's Magazine* in April, tying for first prize in short story contest. In June submits *K19* to Maxwell Perkins and is persuaded to shelve it. In August moves to 101 Columbia Heights, Brooklyn. Spends Labor Day weekend in Montreal. In October visits father's childhood home in York Springs, Pennsylvania. Also visits Bermuda.

1933   Introduced to Ernest Hemingway by Perkins in January. Accompanies Perkins to Johns Hopkins Hospital and visits sister Mabel in Washington. Finishes *No Door*, a short novel, in February. Attends March 4 inauguration of Franklin D. Roosevelt in Washington, D.C. In March, *Look Homeward, Angel* published in Germany as *Schau Heimwärts, Engel*. In May visits York Springs and Gettysburg, Pennsylvania, with brother Fred. In July visits Gettysburg with Maxwell Perkins. In August makes first of several visits to Kathleen and Clayton Hoagland in Rutherford, New Jersey. In September visits Vermont with Robert Raynolds, who later writes *Thomas Wolfe:*

Memoir of a Friendship. In October moves to 5 Montague Terrace, Brooklyn. On December 23 delivers to Perkins manuscript of *The October Fair*, part of which is later included in *Of Time and the River*.

1934   In January hires Elizabeth Nowell as literary agent. Through June revises *Of Time and the River*, which is sent to the printer by Maxwell Perkins in July. Works on galleys in August. In September visits World's Fair, Chicago. In October visits Elizabeth Lemmon, a close friend of Maxwell Perkins, at her farm Welbourne in Middleburg, Virginia.

1935   Visited by mother in Brooklyn during January. Sails March 2 on the *Ile de France* for sixth trip to Europe to be away when *Of Time and the River* appears. Arrives in Paris on March 8, the day *Of Time and the River* is published. Receives reassuring cable March 14 from Perkins about critics' reception of the book. Goes to London March 24. Lives at 26 Hanover Square. Arrives in Berlin May 7; is entertained and lionized while traveling through Germany for more than a month. Goes to Denmark June 16 and is treated for a mild venereal infection. Sails June 27 from Bremerhaven on the *Bremen*. Lands July 4 in New York. Goes with Perkins to roof of Prince George Hotel, Brooklyn, top of Radio City, and rooftop restaurant of St. Moritz Hotel, accompanied part of the time by Brenda Jeliffe. Leaves New York July 27 for Colorado after dealing with lawsuit brought by Madeline Boyd for commissions on publications. Lectures at Colorado State College of Education, Greeley, on July 30. Guest Lecturer at Colorado Writers' Conference, Boulder, July 31–August 9. Visits Rocky Mountain National Park with poet Thomas Hornsby Ferril and his wife. Visits Santa Fe and Grand Canyon with Desmond Powell, former New York University colleague. Visits Los Angeles and San Francisco. Meets Jean Harlow in Hollywood. On return trip to New York in September stops in St. Louis to visit house where brother Grover died in 1904. Settles at 865 First Avenue, New York. *From Death to Morning* published November 14. Attends Christmas Eve party with friends from Chapel Hill.

1936   Begins writing *The Vision of Spangler's Paul* in March. *Of Time and the River* published in Germany as *Von Zeit und Strom. The Story of a Novel* published April 21. Argues with Perkins about its price. Attacked by Bernard DeVoto in "Genius Is Not Enough," *Saturday Review of Literature,* April 25. In May settles lawsuit over royalties with Madeline Boyd. In June visits Chicago. Sails July 23 on the *Europa* for seventh and last trip to Europe. In August attends Olympic Games in Berlin. In September has affair with Thea

Voelcker. Sails September 17 for home aboard the *Paris.* Lands September 24 in New York. In October quarrels with Perkins about politics. In November sued for libel by Marjorie Dorman over *No Door,* bringing to a head dissatisfaction with Scribner's. In December meets members of the Southern Agrarians during stop in Richmond, Virginia.

1937   Visits New Orleans January 1–11. Visits Biloxi, Atlanta, and Chapel Hill January 12–30. On February 3 settles Dorman's suit out of court. Ill with the "flu" in March. Rewrites will. In April visits Gettysburg, Pennsylvania, Roanoke and Bristol, Virginia, and Burnsville, North Carolina. Arrives May 3 in Asheville for first visit since publication of *Look Homeward, Angel.* In July rents cabin at Oteen, near Asheville. Leaves Asheville September 5. Visits Anne Armstrong in Bristol, Virginia, September 5–8. Visits Sherwood Anderson in Marion, Virginia, September 8–9. Quarrels with Mrs. Anderson. Break with Scribner's becomes public. In October settles at the Hotel Chelsea, New York, in eighth-floor corner suite. Spends Christmas with family of new editor, Edward Aswell, in Chappaqua, New York. Signs contract with Harper and Brothers on New Year's Eve.

1938   Wins lawsuit February 8 against Murdach Dooher to recover manuscripts. Sees Perkins for last time. Delivers two bundles of manuscript to Edward Aswell on May 17 before leaving New York. Lectures at Purdue University May 19. Visits Chicago May 21 and then takes train for Denver. After a week in Denver, arrives in Portland, Oregon, June 7. Journeys by car June 20–July 2 through the Western national parks. Falls ill July 8 in Seattle. Hospitalized by Dr. Edward C. Ruge in Firlawns, his private sanatorium in Kenmore, north of Seattle. Transferred August 6 to Providence Hospital, Seattle. Writes last letter August 12, a note to Perkins. Leaves Seattle by train September 6 for Johns Hopkins Hospital, Baltimore. Operation on September 12 at Johns Hopkins by Dr. Walter Dandy reveals incurable miliary tuberculosis of the brain. Dies September 15 at Johns Hopkins Hospital. Buried at Riverside Cemetery, Asheville.

1939   *The Web and the Rock* published June 22.

1940   *You Can't Go Home Again* published September 18.

1941   *The Hills Beyond* published October 15.

Selected Bibliography

Books by Thomas Wolfe

Look Homeward, Angel: A Story of the Buried Life. New York: Charles Scribner's Sons, 1929.

Of Time and the River: A Legend of Man's Hunger in His Youth. New York: Charles Scribner's Sons, 1935.

From Death to Morning. New York: Charles Scribner's Sons, 1935.

The Story of a Novel. New York: Charles Scribner's Sons, 1936.

The Web and the Rock. New York: Harper & Brothers, 1939.

You Can't Go Home Again. New York: Harper & Brothers, 1940.

The Hills Beyond. New York: Harper & Brothers, 1941.

Selected Magazine Publications of Thomas Wolfe

"An Angel on the Porch." *Scribner's Magazine* 86 (August 1929): 205–10.

"A Portrait of Bascom Hawke." *Scribner's Magazine* 91 (April 1932): 193–98, 239–56.

"The Web of Earth." *Scribner's Magazine* 92 (July 1932): 1–5, 43–64.

"The House of the Far and Lost." *Scribner's Magazine* 96 (August 1934): 71–81.

"I Have a Thing to Tell You." *New Republic* 90 (March 10, 1937): 132–36; (March 17, 1937): 159–64; (March 24, 1937): 202–7.

"The Lost Boy." *Redbook Magazine* 70 (November 1937): 25–28, 80–90. Rpt. *The Lost Boy.* Edited by James W. Clark, Jr. Chapel Hill: University of North Carolina Press, 1992.

"The Party at Jack's." *Scribner's Magazine* 105 (May 1939): 14–16, 40, 42–49, 58–62.

Letters and Notebooks

Cargill, Oscar, and Thomas Clark Pollock, eds. *The Correspondence of Thomas Wolfe and Homer Andrew Watt*. New York: New York University Press, 1954.

Holman, C. Hugh, and Sue Fields Ross, eds. *The Letters of Thomas Wolfe to His Mother*. Chapel Hill: University of North Carolina Press, 1968.

Kennedy, Richard S., ed. *Beyond Love and Loyalty: The Letters of Thomas Wolfe and Elizabeth Nowell*. Chapel Hill: University of North Carolina Press, 1983.

Kennedy, Richard S., and Paschal Reeves, eds. *The Notebooks of Thomas Wolfe*. Chapel Hill: University of North Carolina Press, 1970.

Nowell, Elizabeth, ed. *The Letters of Thomas Wolfe*. New York: Charles Scribner's Sons, 1956.

Stutman, Suzanne, ed. *My Other Loneliness: Letters of Thomas Wolfe and Aline Bernstein*. Chapel Hill: University of North Carolina Press, 1983.

————. *Holding on for Heaven: The Cables and Postcards of Thomas Wolfe and Aline Bernstein*. N.p.: Thomas Wolfe Society, 1985.

Terry, John Skally, ed. *Thomas Wolfe's Letters to His Mother*. New York: Charles Scribner's Sons, 1943.

Wolfe, Thomas. *A Western Journal: A Daily Log of the Great Parks Trip*. Pittsburgh: University of Pittsburgh Press, 1951.

Biographies

Adams, Agatha Boyd. *Thomas Wolfe: Carolina Student, a Brief Biography*. Chapel Hill: University of North Carolina Library, 1950.

Austin, Neal F. *A Biography of Thomas Wolfe*. Austin, Tex.: Roger Beacham, 1968.

Boyd, Madeline. *Thomas Wolfe: The Discovery of a Genius*. Edited by Aldo P. Magi. N.p.: Thomas Wolfe Society, 1981.

Donald, David Herbert. *Look Homeward: A Life of Thomas Wolfe*. Boston: Little, Brown and Co., 1987.

Evans, Elizabeth. *Thomas Wolfe*. New York: Ungar, 1984.

Kennedy, Richard S. *The Window of Memory: The Literary Career of Thomas Wolfe*. Chapel Hill: University of North Carolina Press, 1962.

Klein, Carole. *Aline*. New York: Harper & Row, 1979.

McElderry, Bruce R., Jr. *Thomas Wolfe*. New York: Twayne Publishers, 1964.

Norwood, Hayden. *The Marble Man's Wife*. New York: Charles Scribner's Sons, 1947.

Nowell, Elizabeth. *Thomas Wolfe*. New York: Doubleday and Co., 1960.

Raynolds, Robert. *Thomas Wolfe: Memoir of a Friendship*. Austin: University of Texas Press, 1964.

Turnbull, Andrew. *Thomas Wolfe*. New York: Charles Scribner's Sons, 1968.

Walser, Richard. *Thomas Wolfe Undergraduate.* Durham: Duke University Press, 1977.

Walser, Richard, ed. *The Enigma of Thomas Wolfe: Biographical and Critical Selections.* Cambridge: Harvard University Press, 1953.

Wheaton, Mabel Wolfe, and LeGette Blythe. *Thomas Wolfe and His Family.* Garden City, N.Y.: Doubleday and Co., 1961.

Bibliographies

Holman, C. Hugh. "Thomas Wolfe: A Bibliographical Study." *Texas Studies in Literature and Language* 1 (Autumn 1959): 427–45.

Johnson, Elmer D. *Of Time and Thomas Wolfe: A Bibliography, with a Character Index of His Works.* New York: Scarecrow Press, 1959.

———. *Thomas Wolfe: A Checklist.* Kent: Kent State University Press, 1970.

Johnston, Carol. *Thomas Wolfe: A Descriptive Bibliography.* Pittsburgh: University of Pittsburgh Press, 1987.

Phillipson, John S. *Thomas Wolfe: A Reference Guide.* Boston: G. K. Hall, 1977.

Preston, George R. *Thomas Wolfe: A Bibliography.* New York: Charles Boesen, 1943.

Teicher, Morton I. "A Bibliography of Books with Selections by Thomas Wolfe." *Bulletin of Bibliography* 38 (October–December 1981): 194–208

Books by Aline Bernstein

Three Blue Suits. New York: Equinox Cooperative Press, 1933.
The Journey Down. New York: Alfred A. Knopf, 1938.
An Actor's Daughter. New York: Alfred A. Knopf, 1941.
Miss Condon. New York: Alfred A. Knopf, 1947.

Secondary Sources Cited

Aswell, Edward C. "A Note on Thomas Wolfe." In *The Hills Beyond* by Thomas Wolfe. New York: Harper & Brothers, 1948.

Bergreen, Laurence. *James Agee.* New York: Penguin Books, 1985.

Charters, Ann. *Kerouac.* San Francisco: Straight Arrow Books, 1973.

DeVoto, Bernard. "Genius Is Not Enough." *Saturday Review of Literature* 13 (April 25, 1936): 3–4, 14–15.

Field, Leslie. *Thomas Wolfe and His Editors.* Norman: University of Oklahoma Press, 1987.

Fremont-Smith, Eliot. "Wolfegate: Of Time, the River, and Fraud." *Village Voice,* February 25–March 3, 1981, pp. 35, 37.

Garrett, George. *James Jones*. San Diego: Harcourt Brace Jovanovich, 1984.

Halberstadt, John. "The Making of Thomas Wolfe's Posthumous Novels." *Yale Review* 70 (Autumn 1980): 79–99.

Hoagland, Clayton and Kathleen. *Thomas Wolfe Our Friend, 1933–1938*. Athens, Ohio: Croissant and Co., 1979.

Jones, Howard Mumford. "Thomas Wolfe's Short Stories." *Saturday Review of Literature* 13 (November 30, 1935): 13.

Kennedy, Richard. "The Wolfegate Affair." *Harvard Magazine* 84 (September–October 1981): 48–53.

Mailer, Norman. *Advertisements for Myself*. New York: New American Library, 1959.

Marx, Samuel. *Thomas Wolfe and Hollywood*. Athens, Ohio: Croissant and Co., 1980.

Mitgang, Herbert. *Dangerous Dossiers*. New York: Donald I. Fine, 1988.

Roberts, David. *Jean Stafford*. Boston: Little, Brown and Co., 1988.

Saal, Rollene W. "Pick of the Paperbacks." *Saturday Review of Literature*, October 23, 1965, p. 62.

Winter, Ella. *And Not to Yield*. New York: Harcourt Brace and World, 1963.

Index